OPEN CARRY HANDBOOK

MICHIGAN
2011
EDITION

www.citizensleaguesd.com

LEGAL DISCLAIMER

The author and editors of this book have made every attempt to ensure that the information presented in this book is accurate. Whenever it seemed necessary, laws, Attorney General opinions and case law were consulted. However, courts make rulings every day, and laws are virtually always in a state of flux. Thus, we make no guarantee that anything in this book is correct. Don't forget that missing even one small detail could cost you your freedom or your life. This isn't a subject to be taken lightly.

With this in mind, this book cannot be considered legal advice. No guarantees are made that you will be safe from prosecution or other legal action should you choose to open carry (or do anything else discussed in this book). Just because it is mentioned in this book does not mean it will work in court.

Those who have worked on this book accept no liability, legal or otherwise, for any issues that readers of this book may encounter as a result of the information presented here.

TABLE OF CONTENTS

FOREWARD

This book was written as a guide for responsibly open carrying a holstered handgun in the state of Michigan. It is clear that open carry (OC) is not for everyone. Family situations, job issues and so on can make OC difficult and/or impractical. Each person must individually decide whether OC is right for him/herself.

Deciding to carry a firearm for self-defense is a huge responsibility. The writers recommend that every person interested in OC take a firearm safety course and engage in safe firearm practices at all times.

A few other notes of caution are in order. First, readers who are unfamiliar with analyzing laws are bound to be confused as they try to make sense of Michigan's rather absurd gun laws. It is paramount to remember that in Michigan, as in many states, gun laws are largely archaic remnants of racism. They were enacted under the influence of racist organizations such as the KKK that wished to prevent blacks from being able to legally have weapons. Gun laws were as much about hatred, fear and obsessive control then as they are today.

Trying to use logic to understand bigotry serves no purpose because bigotry in and of itself is illogical. It is import to read and understand the legal details presented here, but trying to make sense of the laws as a whole would be impossible.

Law enforcement agents may be taken aback by the large portion of the book that is dedicated to handling unlawful police abuse. This is not intended as a sign of hostility toward the police. However, to achieve the level of acceptance that open carriers currently enjoy, we have had to regularly deal with police abuse.

With the woefully inadequate and inaccurate open carry training that has been presented to many police departments across the state up to this point, we would be remiss if we did not place heavy emphasis on how to handle police encounters.

Perhaps one day soon, police across Michigan will be properly educated and trained in regard to open carrying, and they will respect open carriers as fellow citizens.

THANK YOU

Sincere gratitude goes out to everyone who made this book possible. Everyone who has been screamed at, detained, arrested and falsely prosecuted by government agents as a result of open carrying is owed a tremendous thank you from anyone who values freedom in Michigan.

Without the selfless efforts of everyone who open carried in the face of this abuse, this book wouldn't be possible, and law-abiding Michigan residents would not be able safely and confidently exercise their Constitutionally protected freedoms to the extent they now can.

Also worthy of commendation are the lawyers who have worked at reduced costs or for free to provide legal counsel for open carriers who have been victims of government abuse. Most notably, Dean Greenblatt defended OCDO member TheSzerdi for the token price of 1000 rounds of ammunition when he was falsely accused of a crime by the city of Detroit.

Last, but not least, every police officer and other public official who has worked with us to end the harassment of those who choose to legally carry weapons. We thank you for serving and protecting us.

THE FOUR RULES OF GUN SAFETY

No matter how experienced you are with firearms, or how safely you feel you use them, no responsible armed person can ever lose sight of the fact that weapons can instantly end lives. Before discussing open carry, we will address the four rules of gun safety.

Rule #1: CONSIDER EVERY FIREARM TO BE LOADED.

Rule #2: ALWAYS KEEP YOUR FINGER OFF OF THE TRIGGER UNTIL YOU ARE IN THE ACT OF FIRING.

Rule #3: NEVER ALLOW THE MUZZLE TO COVER ANYTHING YOU AREN'T WILLING TO DESTROY.

Rule #4: ALWAYS BE SURE OF YOUR TARGET AND WHAT IS BEYOND IT.

Open Carry Pictures

CHAPTER 1

HISTORY OF MODERN OPEN CARRY IN MICHIGAN

In 2004, John Pierce and Mike Stollenwerk founded the nationwide Internet forum www.opencarry.org (OCDO) to promote gun rights and the right to openly carry a handgun.

In December 2007, the first meeting of Michigan OCDO members occurred in Brighton, Michigan. Four people, three of them open carrying, met at a local McDonald's.

By the spring of 2008, Michigan gun owners choosing to open carry began to become more common and organized, most often through OCDO.

Fast forward to 2011, and Michigan OCDO members have become a formidable group of people who have educated many thousands of Michigan police officers and citizens. They have also been the focus of dozens of news stories throughout the state. The open carry movement grows stronger by the day, and we hope you'll join us, if you're up to the task.

Second ever open carry meeting in Michigan, at a McDonalds in Flint, March 2008.

John Roshek, President, Citizens League for Self Defense, Inc., (CLSD) giving an open carry seminar at the Gander Mountain in Utica, Michigan, 2010.

OCDO member Jeff Sayers during a Fox 2 interview on open carry.

CHAPTER 2

YOUR RIGHTS UNDER STATE AND FEDERAL LAW

By Federal and Michigan state law, anyone 18 and older with no criminal convictions can buy, own and carry rifles, shotguns and handguns. However, according to Federal law, 18 to 20 year olds can only buy handguns from private individuals if allowed by state law, which is the case in Michigan. By Federal law, 21 is the minimum age to buy a handgun from a Federal Firearms License (FFL) dealer. Long guns are legal to buy for anyone age 18 years or older.

If you would like to own a firearm but aren't sure if you are legally able to do so because of citizenship status or past criminal convictions, you may call the FBI to ask to have yourself checked with the National Instant Check System (NICS), a mandatory check used for all purchases of firearms from FFL-holding gun dealers. The telephone number is (304) 625-3878.

If you find out that you are ineligible due to a criminal record, you may be able to have your record expunged, after which you would be able to legally own firearms again.

This is an expensive process that does not always work. If you need to do this, find a good lawyer, and be ready to pay a substantial amount of money.

In the past, a local unit of government in Michigan had complete discretion in making rules or regulations in regard to firearms possession and carry. Even if state law allowed the ownership and/or carry of a certain type of firearm, a city or town could easily ban it. This, however, changed in 1990, when Michigan lawmakers passed MCL 123.1102 (Exhibit 1 A), commonly called the "preemption law" because it preemptively stops local units of government from restricting firearm possession and ammunition.

MCL 123.1102 states, in pertinent part: *A local unit of government shall not impose special taxation on, enact or enforce any ordinance or regulation pertaining to, or regulate in any other manner the ownership, registration, purchase, sale, transfer, transportation, or possession of pistols or other firearms, ammunition for pistols or other firearms, or components of pistols or other firearms, except as otherwise provided by federal law or a law of this state.*

123.1102 was upheld in 2003 when the Michigan Coalition of Responsible Gun Owners (MCRGO) took on the city of Ferndale's defiance of the law in the court case MCRGO v Ferndale.

(Exhibit 1 D) The Michigan Supreme Court upheld that cities and towns, including Ferndale, have no right to restrict gun rights beyond state law.

Some cities and towns have neglected to take illegal ordinances off the books after this law was passed. As a result, many law-abiding Michigan gun owners have taken it upon themselves to inform city councils of their illegal ordinances. Due to the efforts of open carriers throughout the state, many of these ordinances have removed.

Further demonstrating that law-abiding citizens of Michigan have the right to arm themselves is Michigan's State Constitution. Article 1, Section 6 states that "Every person has the right to bear arms for defense of himself and the state."

There is also the Second Amendment to the US Constitution, which most readers are already familiar with: *A well regulated militia being necessary to the security of a free state, the right of the people to keep and bear arms shall not be infringed.*

When the Second Amendment was written, there was very widespread understanding that the militia included all able-bodied males and that "well regulated" meant "to work as expected."

Today, the National Guard, although much newer than the Bill of Rights, is wrongly believed by many to be the militia, and "well regulated" is believed to warrant the restriction of gun rights past wit's end through bureaucratic laws. Even if the Second Amendment was only to protect the rights of militants, which it's not, United States Code Title 10, Subtitle A, Chapter 13, § 311 defines able bodied adult males age 17 to 44 as the unorganized militia.

It is abundantly clear that the Second Amendment means that because a population of proficiently armed adults is **_necessary_** to keep a state free and secure, the **_people's_** right to own and carry guns cannot be infringed.

It does not say that the right of a militia to keep and bear arms shall not be infringed; the militia is mentioned only as an explanation of the justification that people be armed.

In June 2010, the Supreme Court of the United States (SCOTUS) ruled with the McDonald v Chicago case that the Second Amendment does indeed apply to the states and not simply the Federal government.

In the years to follow this case, more lawsuits will be filed across the country, and further restorations of gun rights across the country will take place, perhaps even in Michigan.

As of this writing, the attorney who worked on both McDonald v Chicago and Heller v DC is working on a suit against Maryland for not issuing carry permits to everyone who is legally eligible, which could potentially lead to SCOTUS-mandated 50 states shall issue. It is an exciting time for gun rights in the US.

CHAPTER 3

OPEN CARRY <u>WITHOUT</u> A CONCEALED PISTOL LICENSE

If you are a Michigan resident 18 years or older and do not have a CPL but have a pistol registered in your name, you may carry it openly almost anywhere besides court buildings, Federal buildings, theaters, post offices, casinos, sports arenas, day care centers, banks and financial institutions, hospitals, churches or other houses of worship, school property, vehicles of any kind, any establishment that has a liquor license, the sterile areas of airports and any private property that the owners or agents of the owners do not want you on.

If you are from another state, you MUST have a license to purchase, carry, possess or transport a pistol if you choose to legally carry a pistol in Michigan, which is discussed in much greater detail in Chapter 5. Unlike the less strict Federal law that says a pistol is under 26", MCL 750.222 (Exhibit 2A) defines a pistol as any firearm under 30" in length. In pertinent part, 750.222 says:

<u>(e) "Pistol" means a loaded or unloaded firearm that is 30 inches or less in length, or a loaded or unloaded firearm that by its construction and appearance conceals itself as a firearm.</u>

MCL 750.234d and MCL 750.237a (Exhibits 3A and 4A) list some of the places that non-CPL holders cannot carry. The laws do not make a distinction between the parking areas and the buildings themselves. Without a license to carry concealed, do not set foot anywhere on the property of these locations while OCing. Even having a pistol in your trunk at one of these locations could theoretically land you in legal trouble.

A common misconception held by many police officers is that the highly unconstitutional Federal Gun Free School Zones Act (GFSZA, Exhibit 1 D) of 1996 prohibits non-CPL holders from carrying their registered handguns openly within 1000 feet of a K-12 school. However, this is incorrect.

MCL 28.422 (Exhibit 5 A) describes Michigan's pistol registration process as a "license to carry." The GFSZA exempts those who are licensed to carry by their home state. In effect, this eliminates this Federal law from being a concern to a non-CPL-holding Michigan OCer within 1000 feet of a school carrying a registered (to them) handgun.

Individuals who do not hold a CPL but are openly carrying their properly registered handgun can be as close to a K-12 school as they wish, as long as they do not actually set foot on the property of the school.

MCL 750.234d states that an exemption to the restrictions stipulated therein is *(d) A person who possesses a firearm on the premises of an entity described in subsection (1) if that possession is with the permission of the owner or an agent of the owner of that entity.* Therefore, you may OC in these places without a

CPL if you have permission. If you choose to OC in this context, it would be wise to obtain permission in writing as an added precaution and keep copies.

TRANSPORT OF HANDGUNS BY NON-CPL HOLDERS

There is substantial confusion about how to transport a handgun in a motor vehicle in Michigan without a CPL.

Much of this is because the law changed in 2002 with the passage of MCL 750.231a (Exhibit 7 A), which allows non-CPL holders to transport their pistols for all lawful purposes as long as they are unloaded, kept in a case designed for firearms and placed in a trunk or back area that is inaccessible to the occupants of the vehicle. Before the passage of this law, there were only seven circumstances in which non-CPL holders could transport their handguns. Confusion still lingers over the transportation of handguns because the lawmakers drafting this legislation left in the original seven circumstances but used the word "includes" to indicate that the list is partial, not complete.

As long as you are not breaking any other laws, this law poses no restrictions on non-CPL holders transporting unloaded and cased pistols in their trunks, or other inaccessible parts of a vehicle with no trunk, such at the bed of a truck, or the very back of a van.

(b) "Lawful purpose" includes the following:
(vii)While en route to or from a hunting or target

shooting area.

(ii) While transporting a pistol en route to or from his or her home or place of business and place of repair.

(iii) While moving goods from 1 place of abode or business to another place of abode or business.

(iv) While transporting a licensed pistol en route to or from a law enforcement agency or for the purpose of having a law enforcement official take possession of the weapon.

(v) While en route to or from his or her abode or place of business and a gun show or places of purchase or sale.

(vi) While en route to or from his or her abode to a public shooting facility or public land where discharge of firearms is permitted by law, rule, regulation, or local ordinance.

(vii) While en route to or from his or her abode to a private property location where the pistol is to be used as is permitted by law, rule, regulation, or local ordinance.

One handy solution that non-CPL-holding Michigan open carriers have been doing for years is to allow a CPL holder to take temporary possession of their handguns while inside of a motor vehicle. This is legal by Act 75 of 2006 (Exhibit 7 A), which amended MCL 28.432 to specify that Sections 1, 2 and 9 of MCL 28.422 (a law that would otherwise still outlaw borrowing pistols) do not apply to: *An individual carrying, possessing, using, or transporting a pistol belonging to another individual, if the other individual's pistol is properly licensed and inspected under this act and the individual carrying, possessing, using, or transporting the pistol has obtained a license under section 5b to carry a concealed pistol.*

Note that CPL holders may borrow handguns registered in Michigan from CPL and non-CPL holders alike. Non-CPL holders would be committing a crime under MCL28.432 if they borrowed a handgun.

MCL 750.227 (Exhibit 21 A), in pertinent part, says the following:

750.227 Concealed weapons; carrying; penalty.
Sec. 227.

(2) A person shall not carry a pistol concealed on or about his or her person, **or, whether concealed or otherwise, in a vehicle operated or occupied by the person**, *except in his or her dwelling house, place of business, or on other land possessed by the person, without a license to carry the pistol as provided by law and if licensed, shall not carry the pistol in a place or manner inconsistent with any restrictions upon such license.*

Note that Section .227 does not define vehicles or the meaning of "in a vehicle," and definitions of vehicles from other laws do not have any bearing on this law. This is why bicycle, horse, motorcycle and snowmobile carry are considered gray areas. Non-CPL holders are strongly advised not to open carry while in or on ANY type of vehicle.

CHAPTER 4

OPEN CARRY <u>WITH</u> A CONCEALED PISTOL LICENSE

In Michigan, if you have a CPL or a home state equivalent license to carry concealed and you are willing to carry openly, you actually have fewer restrictions on carrying a pistol than in almost any other state.

On the back of a CPL, there is a list of places that a holder cannot carry <u>concealed</u>. However, a CPL holder is legally able to carry <u>openly</u> in most of these places, at least those that are listed under MCL 28.425o. All that's restricted from open carry for CPL holders is private property where the owners do not want you and Federal buildings, post offices, casinos, courts, sterile areas of airports and some reservation land, depending on the reservation. Always look up reservation laws ahead of time before carrying there.

In addition, there has been an absurd and baseless rumor going around for years that a concealed pistol license mandates that you carry concealed. <u>There is no such law!</u>

Many CPL holders are surprised when they learn that they can carry openly at *almost* all of the places that the back of their CPL lists that they can't carry concealed. MCL 28.425o (Exhibit 19 A) restricts only concealed carry, and MCL 750.234d and MCL 750.237 (Exhibits

3 A and 4 A) both exempt CPL holders. But it's a fact, so long as you don't get kicked off of private property or asked to leave a government-run facility you have no right to be at, like an elementary school.

If you OC in one of these places restricted under your CPL, you'll want to dress in a way to ensure you aren't even partially concealing. Also remember that you don't want to use an inside-the-waistband (IWB) holster with only the top half tucked out. There is no case law to protect this as open carry; in addition, IWB OC is a bad option because of the lack of retention that IWB holsters have. There is, however, an Attorney General (AG) opinion #3158 (Exhibit 1 B) that protects regular holstered carry as being open and legal. In pertinent part, it states:

"I am, therefore, of the opinion that if a pistol is carried in a holster or belt, on the outside of the clothing so as to be in plain view, it does not constitute carrying a concealed weapon.

If it is worn under a coat, it would be, in my judgment, a violation of the statute, as the same would then not be in plain view."

Another AG opinion, #7097 of 2002 (Exhibit 2 B), further demonstrated the legality of a CPL holder OCing in a concealed carry free zone. 7097 states in pertinent part:

"By its express terms, section 234d prohibits certain persons from carrying a firearm in the enumerated

places but explicitly exempts from its prohibition "[a] person licensed by this state or another state to carry a concealed weapon." Thus, any person licensed to carry a concealed pistol, including a private investigator, is exempt from the gun-free zone restrictions imposed by section 234d of the Penal Code and may therefore possess firearms while on the types of premises listed in that statute."

Also important to remember is that preemption hasn't been expanded to colleges because Michigan Community Colleges are given sweeping unconstitutional power by the Community Colleges Act (Exhibit 9 A), and so college students can still be expelled for carrying concealed or openly on campus, even if legal according to state law.

CPL holders are often surprised to find out that MCL 28.425f, Michigan's concealed carry disclosure law (Exhibit 10 A), provides no obligation to disclose anything while on foot OCing and not CCing a backup, nor does any other law. Mandatory CPL holder disclosure applies only to carrying concealed or carrying under the authority of a CPL in a vehicle, or to non-residents in some other circumstances, which is covered later in the non-resident chapter.

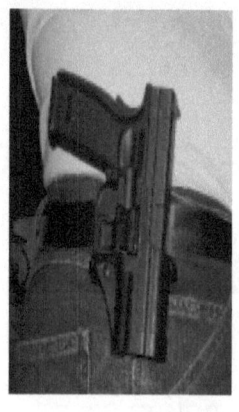  

| Clear open carry with a retention holster. | Arguably concealed carry with an IWB holster. | Definitely legal OWB open carry with an IWB holster, which is not secure. |

Something usually covered by CPL classes, but worth mentioning here again, is that MCL 750.227c (Exhibit 11 A) prohibits the carry of any loaded firearms other than a pistol in a vehicle.

It makes no exemptions for CPL holders. CPLs in Michigan cover only the carry of firearms that Michigan defines as pistols, and nothing else.

CARRYING LEGALITY QUICK REFERENCE CHART
(Courtesy of OCDO member WARCHILD)
Continued on the next page

Carry A Firearm - With Or Without CPL	Yes-Y	No-N
This chart is not all inclusive. If you have a specfic question that is not covered here, research further.		
Concealed Carry w/o CPL		
CC On your own property	Y	
CC Outside your property		N
OC W/O CPL		
A bank or financial institution		N
A church or other house of religious worship		N
A court		N
A theatre		N
A sports arena		N
A day care center		N
A hospital		N
A school (K-12)		N
Casino		N
Any establishment licensed by the Mich liquor act		N
You can OC without a CPL in any of the places listed in .234d with permission of the owner.	Y	
CC W/CPL		
A federal reserve bank		N
A private owned bank or financial institution	Y	
A church or other house of religious worship (with church officials permission)	Y	N
A court		N
A theatre (more than 2500 seating capacity)		N
A sports arena (more than 2500 seating capacity)		N
A day care center		N
A hospital		N
A school (K-12)		N
Casino		N
OC W/CPL		
A bank or financial institution	Y	
A church or other house of religious worship	Y	
A court		N
A theatre	Y	
A sports arena	Y	
A day care center	Y	
A hospital	Y	
A school (K-12)	Y	
Casino		N
Any establishment licensed by the Mich liquor act- In any business where the primary souce of income is sold by the glass for consumption on the premisis.		
CC W/CPL: 1. Any business licensed by the Mich. Liquor act: -Majority of income from open glass sales.		N
CC W/CPL: 2.Any business licensed by the Mich. Liquor act: -Majority of income from non-alcohol sales.	Y	
OC W/CPL: 1. Any business licensed by the Mich. Liquor act: -Majority of income from open glass sales.	Y	
OC W/CPL: 2.Any business licensed by the Mich. Liquor act: -Majority of income from non-alcohol sales.	Y	
Required to disclose CC to law enforcement	Y	
OC / CC in National & State Parks & Recreational Areas have some restrictions	Y	
Any business posted: No weapons or firearms. Violation of this posting could result in a trespass charge if you refuse to leave the premisis.		N

CHAPTER 5

NON-RESIDENT CARRY IN MICHIGAN

Non-residents have several options to legally carry pistols in Michigan. Something that fits the description of a license to carry, possess, transport, or purchase will suffice as defined by MCL 28.422. This does not necessarily mean a concealed carry license, but rather a home state license to do at least one of those things listed above, similar to Michigan's registration process. One example would be an Illinois FOID card.

A home state license or permit to carry concealed, if recognized by Michigan for carrying concealed, will grant non-residents all of the same rights in Michigan that a resident CPL holder has.

The last option, and the only option for residents of states with no carry licenses or permits whatsoever, is to obtain an out-of-state license to CC, such as a Wisconsin or California resident obtaining a Utah or Florida permit. MCL 28.422 would appear to render non-resident permits and licenses useless, until you read MCL 28.432, which specifically exempts from 28.422's restrictions US citizens holding a license to carry a concealed pistol from another state. But concealment is still illegal without a home state concealed carry license, as all that this does is satisfy the requirement to have the license to purchase, possess, transport or carry (as is the case with Michigan registration).

So, for example, a Wisconsin resident can't carry pistols in Michigan without a license from another state, but an Illinois resident who has a pistol and a FOID card could come to Michigan and experience a whole lot of newfound freedom to carry with the same rights as a Michigan resident with a registered handgun and no CPL.

Remember: as was covered earlier, if you wish to carry in a restricted area as defined by MCL 28.425o, non-residents must have a resident license to carry concealed, and they can then carry openly. Otherwise, they can carry concealed with permission (preferably in writing) or carry openly with permission as a holder of a state license to purchase, carry, possess and transport but not conceal.

28.422 also requires non-residents to possess their licenses while carrying and show them when asked by law enforcement. Since 28.432 exempts concealed carry license holders from 28.422's stipulations, those with non-resident out-of-state CC licenses don't need to show any ID for OCing, but an out-of-stater with a license that doesn't allow concealment in the state of issuance is required to show the license when asked by law enforcement.

Remember, if you have an out-of-state license or permit to carry concealed and wish to carry concealed in Michigan, MCL 750.231a requires the license to be from your home state of residence, and it also requires you to conform to all of the restrictions appearing on the license or have another license without the restrictions.

The license also must fall under the scope of Michigan's reciprocity agreements; otherwise, it will only allow open carry.

NON-RESIDENT LICENSES TO CARRY CONCEALED HELD BY MICHIGAN RESIDENTS

According to the wording of the law, a Michigan resident who has an out-of-state license to carry concealed has all of the same rights to open carry on foot as a anyone with a resident license to carry concealed. MCL 750.234d and MCL 750.237a both list the places that restrict carrying. They exempt people who are licensed by this state **or another state** to carry concealed pistols.

A small number of states will issue licenses to non-resident 18+ year olds who are legally eligible to carry concealed pistols. Having one of these licenses to carry concealed, according to the wording of the law, enables Michigan residents to OC in the places listed in 234d and 237a.

These licenses do nothing to enable car carry or any form of CC because MCL 750.227 (Exhibit 21 A) prohibits vehicle carry and CC without a resident license to carry a concealed pistol.

Since holders of these licenses can't use the licenses to concealed carry or carry in cars in Michigan, there is never a requirement to disclose the licensed status to police or even to possess the license while OCing. For that matter, the possession of any other ID while OCing is never required because disclosure is only related to concealment and vehicles. If you're carrying in a game area under the license, per MCL 324.43510 (Exhibit 23 A), you would be legally required to have the license with you, but there is no law known to the author that mandates that you show it.

As abundantly clear as the law is, there is a potential problem that unfortunately will probably take future case law to resolve.

In 1994, the anti-gun Michigan Attorney General Frank J. Kelly, a man who did much damage to freedom in Michigan, wrote opinion #6798, which specified that the now obsolete and nonexistent may issue laws put a heavy amount of scrutiny on Michigan CPL applicants. The opinion also states that it would be an absurd consequence contrary to legislative intent if out-of-state licenses to carry concealed allowed concealed carry for Michigan residents, and therefore, carrying under such a license is illegal for Michigan residents.

Opinion #6758 is listed in its entirety in the Appendix for those who wish to make up their own minds in regard to carrying openly under an out-of-state license. The legally safest option is not to do it, even though OCing under such a license appears solidly legal, particularly if you're a dedicated activist with pockets deep enough to fund an extensive legal battle.

CHAPTER 6

WHAT ABOUT BRANDISHING, DISORDERLY CONDUCT AND DISTURBING THE PEACE?

If you don't look into the fine print of the laws, it would seem that you could get charged with and convicted of a generic catch-all bad behavior law, or maybe brandishing, while OCing. But when you actually look at the laws, it doesn't work that way.

Michigan's disorderly conduct charge is found under MCL 750.167 (Exhibit 12 A). It wouldn't hurt to read it, but the main thing is to understand that it is not applicable to OCing. Neither disturbing the peace nor disorderly conduct are even related to guns.

Brandishing could have been an issue, had it not been for Attorney General Jennifer Granholm's opinion # 7101 (Exhibit 3 B), which explicitly defines what brandishing is and then goes on to give an example of what it isn't. In pertinent part, 7101 states:

"In the absence of any reported Michigan appellate court decisions defining "brandishing," it is appropriate to rely upon dictionary definitions.

People v Denio, 454 Mich 691, 699; 564 NW2d 13 (1997). According to The American Heritage Dictionary, Second College Edition

(1982), at p 204, the term brandishing is defined as: "1. To wave or flourish menacingly, as a weapon. 2. To display ostentatiously. –n. A menacing or defiant wave or flourish." This definition comports with the meaning ascribed to this term by courts of other jurisdictions. For example, in United States v Moerman, 233 F3d 379, 380 (CA 6, 2000), the court recognized that in federal sentencing guidelines, "brandishing" a weapon is defined to mean "that the weapon was pointed or waved about, or displayed in a threatening manner."

Applying these definitions to your question, it is clear that a reserve police officer, regardless whether he or she qualifies as a "peace officer," when carrying a handgun in a holster in plain view, is not waving or displaying the firearm in a threatening manner. Thus, such conduct does not constitute brandishing a firearm in violation of section 234e of the Michigan Penal Code.

It is my opinion, therefore, that a reserve police officer, by carrying a handgun in a holster that is in plain view, does not violate section 234e of the Michigan Penal Code,

which prohibits brandishing a firearm in public."

Clearly, brandishing is not an applicable charge for someone lawfully carrying a handgun in a holster.

CHAPTER 7

CARRYING A QUALITY HANDGUN

A modern automatic pistol will have a system that blocks the firing pin or striker with a slide-mounted firing pin or striker block unless the trigger is pulled. Modern hammer-actuated automatics will also have mechanisms to prevent the hammer from touching the firing pin unless the trigger is pulled.

It is very important for any semi-automatic pistol to have both of these features, aside from arguably a traditional 1911 or other single action-only pistol, which may be carried safely with the hammer cocked back and the safety on or the hammer securely at a half-cocked state, as the firing pin in either case is shielded from being hit due to the position of the secured hammer and the contour of the slide. Remember, some pistols may seem to fit this category but actually don't. The most notable example is possibly the CZ52.

Four people known to the author have been injured severely when a CZ52 fell to the ground or the hammer was brushed up against while holstered; the gun discharged because of a cheap sear that quickly wore out and no slide-mounted firing pin block. Always be extremely careful, and be certain that any gun that you carry chambered is safe. Otherwise, it must be carried with an empty chamber.

Such safety features are somewhat less important with

respect to revolvers, because if they are not drop-safe, the chamber in the cylinder underneath the hammer (commonly called the "active chamber") can simply be kept empty. When the trigger is pulled or the hammer is cocked back, the cylinder rotates, bringing the chamber to the left or right into the path of the firing pin.

In order to safely carry a revolver with a round under the hammer, the revolver must have a frame-mounted firing pin with a trigger-activated firing pin block between the pin and the hammer. Otherwise, the revolver could discharge upon the hammer being negligently struck by any object or upon falling to the ground. Other revolvers such as those made by NAA have a point the hammer rests in between 2 chambers, also allowing full loaded carry.

Remember, if you are buying a gun or considering carrying one you already have, do adequate research to ensure that you can carry it safely.

Many people, including many police officers, get shot by their own guns because they try to catch them when they negligently allow them to fall. Good holsters and proper gun handling will avoid this, but it can still happen. If you have a safe and modern handgun in good working order, it will not discharge from hitting the ground.

A potentially unsafe handgun such as a CZ52 should be carried with the chamber empty, if at all, so that there is no reason to try to catch a non-drop-safe gun.

This is generally accurate information, but different firearms have different safety features and all firearms are unique. Please use extreme caution when handling all firearms.

Attempting to catch any falling gun can result in the trigger negligently being pulled, grossly violating the four rules at a bare minimum. So, if a gun falls, do not try to catch it. Pick it up carefully after it has fallen.

USING A QUALITY HOLSTER

A good holster is no fashion statement. As with anything involving firearms, it is nothing short of a life-and-death decision.

While carrying concealed, any holster that holds a handgun securely enough that it won't fall out will normally suffice. However, while carrying openly, particularly in a heavily-populated area where coming into close proximity with strangers is inevitable, it is crucially important to have a retention holster in case a criminal tries to grab your gun.

At this time, there are no known and well-verified incidents, at least in the US, of non-uniformed private individuals being specifically targeted and victimized by criminals for carrying openly. But, as time goes on and OCing becomes more prevalent, it is bound to happen. This is why there is nearly unanimous agreement that retention holsters are mandatory for safe OCing in urban areas.

A retention holster uses at minimum a thumb break but preferably also a hard-to-figure-out locking mechanism, such as a rotating hood that looks like a cross strap.

There are varying levels of retention. It starts at level 1. Level 1 retention is also known as "passive retention." It is basically non-retention and doesn't truly fit the definition of a retention holster. Under level 1 retention, the gun is held in by pressure and friction by perhaps a snap-in-place cross strap or thumb break, and nothing else. These holsters are largely considered inadequate and unsafe for urban open carry.

The next step up is level 2. Level 2 holsters have one of the above-mentioned locking mechanisms. Level 3 holsters have two locking mechanisms, and level 4 has three.

Level 2 or 3 is widely regarded by police, security and private, non-professional OCers as the minimum level of retention for almost any public OCing. Police officers will at times opt for level 4, but this is because they are likely to find themselves in a fistfight where they don't want to shoot a subject.

In terms of private, non-professional OCers, it is much less likely that an OCer will opt to get in a fistfight when assaulted. In most cases, drawing a firearm on a life-threatening assailant is probably a much more likely and prudent decision for the common man or woman OCing or CCing.

One drawback of retention holsters is that they are harder to draw from than non-retention holsters. Practicing literally thousands of times drawing is the only way to ensure you will be able to draw quickly and smoothly if you have to.

It should be noted that the author wanted to discuss different brands of holsters, but none of the major brand names would grant permission to mention their names, and so they have been left out. Please visit opencarry.org or a uniform store to find out more.

GUN BELTS AND KEEPERS

Whether you're carrying concealed or openly, it is a good idea to consider getting a good-quality gun belt. Regular leather or fake leather pants belts, as well as other lower-end pants belts like canvas belts, may not be able to hold the weight of a medium to full-size handgun. Over time, low-quality belts can easily have their shape distorted by that much weight.

Another disadvantage to using a pants belt for carrying guns is that you have to take your gun and magazine pouches off every time you change.

With a dedicated gun belt, you may simply take your entire rig off and put it back on with the snap of a buckle. While most private OCers don't opt for dedicated gun belts, the vast majority of police and armed security guards use this type of rig. They are available from ten dollars up to over a hundred.

Some have also used leather tool belts as gun belts, which is a good idea, since they typically cost only 5 to 15 dollars, last a long time, and are very sturdy.

Some gun belts have Velcro on the inside and are designed to be worn with a pants belt that has Velcro on the outside so that they stick together. Another way to keep the two belts in line is with keepers, which can be used in conjunction with Velcro. Keepers are little leather or nylon straps with usually, but not always, two snaps.

They simply hold the gun and pants belts together. Some gun belts also incorporate a retention mechanism into their buckle, making it very hard to unbuckle them.

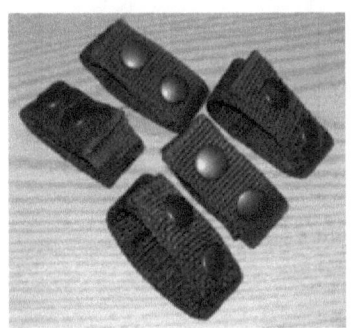

Belt keepers.

Dedicated gun belt, courtesy of Michigander.

Keepers are not always necessary. Pants belts were invented around 1900. Guns have been carried on stand-alone belts for hundreds of years. Much heavier tool belts are carried every day by contractors worldwide with no keepers. Simply taking a gun belt and strapping it around your waist will keep it secure enough for many people.

If you buy a dedicated gun belt, you should try simply putting it on and tightening it up before buying keepers.

If you have trouble with it bouncing around or otherwise bothering you, then inexpensive keepers might be good to try.

Although this can also apply to men, women who use gun belts often have a greater need for keepers because of marginally narrower waists and wider hips, which can cause the belt to ride up their waists, making proper drawing difficult or even impossible without using the non-drawing hand to hold the holster in place.

CHAPTER 8

CARRYING LONG GUNS

Very few people who open carry advocate carrying long guns for general defense in an urban area when handguns may be carried instead. Deadly overpenetration of bullets through walls and other objects is a concern, as is weapon retention and maintaining overall control. No less important is maneuverability inside of a building. Less important, but still a factor, is public perception, which generally isn't favorable when it comes to open carrying a slung shotgun into a business. This is why most consider long guns clumsy and inappropriate for general urban carry.

Using the definition of brandishing that Granholm cited in Opinion #7101 (Exhibit 3 B), one can easily argue that a slung rifle wouldn't be brandishing. However, the opinion certainly provides the more clear-cut example of pistols in holsters. Slung long guns offer more of a risk for a court case. Nevertheless, after a very expensive legal battle, it seems very unlikely that a properly and safely slung rifle or shotgun could be ruled brandishing.

All that said, there are some legitimate reasons to carry a long gun. As per MCL 28.422 (Exhibit 5 A), Michigan law makes legal carry very difficult for someone from a won't issue state like Wisconsin, but no special government permission is needed to carry long guns in most situations.

Also, long gun open carry may appeal to someone 18 to 20 years old who is legally able to obtain a pistol from a private individual but, thanks to Federal law, cannot yet obtain a handgun from a dealer until age 21. People in this age bracket may not have available to them a handgun they wish to buy. However, they may have a 12 gauge or other long gun that they have wish to carry.

Lastly, some people may have a long arm but not enough money to buy a handgun. All of these are arguably legitimate reasons to carry a long gun, despite the controversy it causes.

Looking beyond its controversial nature, there are also legal drawbacks to carrying long guns in Michigan. MCL28.422 defines the act of registering a pistol as being a license to carry. This is important, because it bypasses the federal GFSZA (Exhibit 1E) by exempting from the 1000 foot gun ban rule those who are licensed by their home state to carry whatever firearms they may lawfully carry under their license.

This protection does not protect long gun carry, even if you have a CPL, because there is no Michigan license to carry a long gun.

One way you can legally protect yourself is to take advantage of the fact that MCL 750.222 (Exhibit 2A) defines a pistol as any gun less than 30" in length. If you have a common defensive long gun, like an AK, a pump-action or semi-auto shotgun or any number of other long guns, putting a folding stock or stand-alone pistol grip stock on it to give it a length between 26 and 30" will make it a pistol by Michigan law and a long gun by Federal law. This will give you the protections of being "licensed to carry" as defined by MCL28.422 (Exhibit 5 A), which means that you may carry it like any other pistol without a CPL or under the authority of a CPL if you have one. Many knowledgeable CPL holders do this so that they can legally carry loaded and uncased long guns in their vehicles.

NOTE: If you are going to alter a long gun and register it as a pistol, make very certain that you don't accidentally make it an NFA weapon. Long guns must have an over all length of 26" or more and a barrel length of 18" for shotguns and 16" for rifles to be non-NFA weapons. More information about NFA weapons is included in the NFA chapter of this book.

TRANSPORTING LONG GUNS

MCL 750.227d (Exhibit 13 A) regulates vehicular transporting of long guns in Michigan. There are many misconceptions about this law, but those that have actually read it understand that you don't need to have the ammo in a separate case nor does the long gun have to be in the trunk, as many believe. You could, for example, be driving, have a magazine in your pocket and your rifle in a case next to you on the passenger seat with the bolt locked back so it could be shooting in under two seconds, and you'd be legal. Or you could have the long gun in the front seat unloaded and broken down, with a magazine ready to go. This is a solid self-defense option for those without CPLs, but anyone could still easily be in violation of the GFSZA doing this since there is no license to carry long guns, and the GFSZA requires cased or racked and always locked transport of unlicensed firearms within 1000' of a school.

One concern is MCL 324.43510 (Exhibit 23 A). In pertinent part, it says:

(1) Subject to subsection (2) and except as provided in section 43513, a person shall not carry or transport a firearm, slingshot, bow and arrow, crossbow, or a trap while in any area frequented by wild animals unless that person has in his or her possession a license as required under this part.

43510 is part of the Natural Resources and Environmental Act 451 of 1994 Part 435 Hunting and Fishing Licensing section. So, it would seem that it does not apply to places not open to hunting. However, if you were somewhere open to hunting, you would want a CPL or hunting license as required by 324.43510 (Exhibit 23 A) to carry a long gun while there, and unlike CPLs, Michigan hunting licenses are available to out-of-state residents, albeit at greater cost than to residents.

Evil Creamsicle and his Michigan Pistol registered folding stock WASR10. It's a rifle by Federal law.

CHAPTER 9

STATE PARKS, STATE LAND, NATIONAL PARKS AND NATIONAL FORESTS

Many if not most people who have an interest in firearms have an interest in the outdoors, and this almost inevitably leads to the question of carrying weapons in state and Federally owned public forests.

As you know from the non-resident license chapter, MCL 324.43510 (Exhibit 23 A) prohibits you from carrying in state game areas unless you possess on your person a legal CPL or valid hunting license. In this instance, and in this instance only, a CPL actually enables you to carry rifles legally. The benefit of being in the possession of a hunting license while in areas open to hunting as well as being legally outfitted to hunt (with orange clothes if needed) exempts you from being charged with brandishing under MCL 750.234e (Exhibit 24 A).

As readers may remember from headlines in late 2009 and early 2010, a bill to mandate that carry be allowed carry in National Parks if permitted by state law was signed into law by President Obama, namely, Sec. 512 of P.L. 111-24, (Exhibit 2 E), which states that if a state law poses no objection, firearms may be taken into National Parks and National Wildlife Refuges for the purpose of lawful self defense, as long as no crimes, like poaching, are attempted. Therefore, it is now legal to carry firearms openly with no CPL and concealed pistols with a CPL in National Parks and National Wildlife Refuges in Michigan. Carry into Federal buildings within such parks can still be prohibited.

Another issue of great interest is target shooting. With or without a CPL, it is legal to target shoot on state land, as long as you're shooting at a safe backstop and not endangering or otherwise infringing on the rights of anyone else there.

Even during cold or rainy weather, many Michigan gun owners prefer to shoot on state land because of the vast numbers of overbearing range masters, high range fees, no-rapid-fire rules and other idiotic garbage that plague what seems to be a majority of Michigan ranges. This is why "The Pit," an 85-yard free range on state land in Lapeer County, is so popular.

The Tonto National Forest in Arizona. Image courtesy of Michigander.

CHAPTER 10

OTHER WEAPONS

Nearly anyone who enjoys and respects firearms will see knives as a useful and necessary tool to have for everyday tasks. Some also consider them to be appropriate last-ditch weapons. For one reason or another, most proficient gun owners have an affinity for good knives.

As you can see from Appendix C, which lists Michigan's pertinent non-firearm-specific laws, state law allows most knives to be carried openly for lawful purposes. However, unlike firearms, there is no state preemption of knife laws. Knife laws of cities and towns across the state vary wildly. The worst part is that nearly all are enforceable by state law. At this time, it is ill advised to carry a knife or other non-firearm weapon of any kind while OCing a firearm, particularly if you aren't intimately familiar with the laws of the community you are in.

MCL 750.224 (Exhibit 14 A) bans blackjacks, bludgeons, billy clubs, metal knuckles, tear gas, and sand bags. The good news is that if you are carrying these things concealed and give a police officer neither permission, nor a reasonable, articulateable suspicion (RAS) to search you, the Fourth Amendments Exclusionary Rule may rescue you by rendering the evidence found during the search inadmissible at trial. Any evidence obtained by police illegally is considered "fruit of the poisonous tree" and cannot be used in court. But the bad news about that is that even if you are not convicted, you could still lose a nice knife or other weapon and thousands in attorney fees. It has happened to Michigan OCers numerous times. And again, cities and towns have a dizzying array of enforceable laws about carrying them.

There is also a further concern: if you were attacked while carrying notoriously weak Michigan-legal pepper spray or some other less lethal or non lethal defense object as well as a gun and chose to defend yourself with the gun, killing or maiming an assailant,

A jury might question your choice to defend yourself with the gun as opposed to the less lethal or non-lethal device.

A 6" bladed navaja, courtesy of Michigander.

NFA WEAPONS

NFA weapons are weapons regulated by the National Firearms Act of 1934. This is a tremendously complicated subject, so much so that you could write an entire book about it. In fact, this has already been done by the ATF. Those who have any interest should go to: http://www.atf.gov/publications/download/p/atf-p-5320-8/atf-p-5320-8.pdf and download the ATF's NFA Handbook. Unfortunately, this book is not available in print; because the information changes regularly, the ATF simply updates it electronically as needed.

Aside from short-barreled rifles, short-barreled shotguns and sound suppressors, all of which are illegal in Michigan because of MCL 750.224 and 750.224b (Exhibit 14 A and 15 A), NFA weapons are legal to buy, sell and own in accordance with all Federal laws. Moreover, when banned types of weapons are eligible for Curio and Relic status, they may be owned under a C and R license. Any of these firearms that are under 30" or an AOW-registered "gadget gun" must be registered as a pistol with the state. Properly registered NFA weapons of Michigan pistol size may also be carried as pistols in accordance with state law.

If you want a short-barreled rifle or shotgun, the only realistic legal ways in Michigan to obtain one are to get a registered pre-86 machine gun, on which you can have any barrel length, or to get a rifle-type weapon like an AK that was made at the factory with no butt stock and a pistol length and thus is a true pistol by state and

Federal law. Or, you could also obtain an NFA-registered AOW shotgun that was originally built with no stock (and can never have one installed and remain an AOW) and a short barrel at the factory. These are legal in Michigan but must be registered as pistols; therefore, they can be carried as such.

Mark Cortis of the Wild West Academy shooting a pre-86 M16.

CHAPTER 11

WHY OPEN CARRY?

As discussed earlier, open carry is not for everyone. Those who are on the fence about OC may want to know its advantages.

Open carry gives you a very fast draw, and it is a very strong deterrent against criminals. Many people who have OCed for any length of time, including the author and editors of this book, have experienced the effects of OC on criminals firsthand. It makes low lives with obvious criminal backgrounds and perhaps criminal intentions turn around and go the other way in a big hurry.

There have also been some high-profile examples of OC deterring felons. In one instance, an open carrier was in a bank talking to a teller, and a gun-toting robber came in. The robber saw the OCer and ran the other way. The OCer didn't see the robber until he later watched security footage. In another example, two OCers eating at a Waffle House convinced five men armed with long guns to abandon their plans of holding up the restaurant.

OCing definitely isn't for everyone, and if you aren't completely confident and comfortable doing it, you shouldn't. You may want to open carry at times and at other times conceal, or you may want to always conceal because you don't feel comfortable with open carrying. Most Michigan open carriers have CPLs and vary the amounts of the time they carry concealed versus carry openly. Others support open carrying but choose to always conceal. The open carry crowd doesn't look down on concealed carry; it only wishes to make sure that people know how to safely open carry if they wish to.

PRESENTING A GOOD PUBLIC IMAGE AS AN OPEN CARRIER

Over the past several years, open carriers in Michigan have spent thousands of hours open carrying. Throughout all of this experience, a few things have become very clear about public perceptions of OC.

Most importantly, a good, friendly and outgoing demeanor is the best way to be well received by most people you see while OCing.

If you act nervous or in any way odd, rather than confident and friendly, people will become concerned and sometimes even call the police, if not just think you're another lunatic gun owner. It's your right to be perceived this way, but it doesn't further the cause of gun rights to do this.

Almost as important is the way you dress and groom yourself, with age also being a factor. Time after time, younger people OCing while having a lot of facial hair and sometimes less-than-business-like clothing have caused people who didn't know any better to call the police, which has caused felony stops, wrongful prosecution and court and police harassment before most police were educated on OC.

One of the most glaring examples of facial hair causing grief involves OCDO member TheSzerdi. He dresses well and is quite friendly. However, he used to have a very long goatee and has long has a very sharp-looking handlebar moustache. While a respectable look, it is different from what most people are used to, and so combined with his open-carried 1911, he had a disproportionate number of 911 calls and police incidents back before most PDs were well educated on open carry. While in a perfect world his appearance would not be an issue, this example demonstrates the importance of considering your self-presentation if you choose to OC.

Some OCers may want to dress in shirts advertising their favorite metal band while wearing beat-up pants and a five-day shave. This will definitely cause more people to take issue with you, but if you insist on dressing like this, you can compensate some by carefully watching your demeanor.

Another practice that will make people become abnormally concerned is carrying obnoxiously large weapons, i.e., the already mentioned issue of long gun carry.

Drop-leg holsters have in some cases seemed to generate more 911 calls than other types of holsters, particularly when worn by those already likely to be hassled because of appearance. Nonetheless, they are a superb way to ensure that you don't accidentally conceal or get falsely accused by a cop of concealing. The pros and cons of such a holster should be carefully considered before choosing to use one.

Remember, if you open carry, you are an ambassador for all gun owners. Try to look good and act even better!

CHAPTER 12

HANDLING HOSTILE POLICE INTERACTIONS WHILE OPEN CARRYING

It seems that the worst of the police abuse against open carriers is behind us, but police harassment is nevertheless still possible and thus always something to be prepared for. In the early days when few people open carried and before the hard work of educating law enforcement and the general public had begun, police officers routinely felony-stopped and otherwise harassed open carriers.

With today's technology, most open carriers advocate carrying voice recorders. There has been some disagreement about whether or not it is legal to record being detained by police, but this issue is resolved by referring to MCL 750.539c and 750.539a (Exhibits 16 and 17 A). Together, these two laws ban the use of electronic devices in eavesdropping on private conversations, which means recording or electronically listening in on or broadcasting a private a conversation to which you aren't party. If the police have stopped you, are talking to you and are also recording the stop (which anyone can later obtain with a FOIA), any conversation that ensues is neither private, nor are you eavesdropping on it. To suggest otherwise seems to make no sense.

Michigander of OCDO, sometimes jokingly called "recorder man" by other OCDO members, advocates and practices carrying no less than two recorders and a cell phone at all times while open carrying. At least one of the recorders should be a spy cam. Spy cams are available cheaply from the Internet, and they come in various forms, such as pens, hats, buttons, watches, cigarette lighters, USB sticks and neckties.

The other recorder, Michigander insists, should be easily identifiable. It should preferably be one that can be left on for extended periods of time while open carrying in a situation in which you believe a police interaction (or any other incident requiring recording) could happen. This type of recorder can and has been illegally taken from OCers by police and shut off during illegal Terry stops, but Michigander feels strongly that it is important to let renegade police feel they have stopped any recording of the incident, even though the back-up spy cam(s) continue(s) to record.

Michigander suggests that the cell phone be used to call 911 so that you can ask for the help of the Michigan State Police and the County Sheriff's department if you trust them; in addition, you can later have a 911 tape of the encounter when you FOIA it. You could also ask for the FBI to be sent out for a color of law complaint under Title 18, U.S.C., Section 242, (Exhibit 3 E). The FBI probably wouldn't come out to fulfill your request, but it definitely won't happen if you don't ask. Michigander suggests the phone be set to speaker so that if it has to be dropped during a police assault, it will hopefully continue to function well enough to continue the 911 call.

Some would consider all of these precautions to be a bit over the top, but there has never been a situation in which an OCer has regretted using too many recorders while interacting with hostile police. In Michigander's case, carrying all of this recording gear is a direct response to his experiences being stopped by the police.

If you find yourself in the terrible situation of being stopped and you don't have a recorder, or perhaps your recorder(s) malfunction(s) or get taken by police, you need to make a report on all of the details of the stop as quickly as possible. In this report, you should include, to the best of your ability, detailed information on everything that happened during the encounter. You can use this information along with the police reports that you should FOIA request. Court cases can take months to play out, and if you didn't record the stop, you will not remember all of the details if you don't write them down. This way, even if you forget certain aspects of the encounter, if you write down what you remember immediately after the incident, you can bring this report with you to court and present it as your testimony, much like police do with their reports weeks, months or even years after an incident. Remember too that if you get caught off guard and don't manage to start recording for some time, for example, because police imply that they will shoot you if you move toward your recorder, you should write down a report of the unrecorded portions of the encounter as soon as you can.

If one or more people are with you during an unrecorded police incident, do not talk about the details

with them, since discussing two sides of the incident can skew details, leading to incorrect recollections of what happened. Instead, all individuals involved should make their own reports before discussing the details in order to
preserve maximum accuracy of statements. (As a side note, this same rule applies in other incidents like traffic accidents. Do not talk to witnesses, and tell witnesses not to talk to each other. Individual recollections are very easily skewed by talking.)

The following is an example of how recording equipment may be put to use to protect you from police abuse. It is not based on any specific, actual event; rather, it is based on true events compiled into one story in order to illustrate the ideal procedures to follow during an encounter with police.

> An OCer is out walking for exercise and fresh air; his standard digital recorder is running.
>
> A police car is seen ahead, and it is approaching fast.
>
> The OCer takes out his cell phone, punches in 911 and then scratches his head, activating his hat camera.
>
> The cop car screeches to a halt, and a cop jumps out of the car with his hand on his sidearm, which is in a holster with the hood down. He screams to the OCer to put his hands in the air.

The OCer complies, pushing his phone's send button as his hands go up. He also quickly states that he doesn't consent to being detained or being searched.

The cop tells the OCer to shut the hell up and to keep his hands in the air until backup arrives. Right after he says this, the 911 dispatcher answers and asks for information about the emergency. Hands still in the air while holding his phone, the OCer tells the dispatcher that he is being unlawfully detained by the PD in whatever city or town he is in, and he asks her to send MSP Troopers to the scene so that they can help record the situation and investigate what he believes is an unlawful stop.

Beginning to realize that he has made a mistake, the cop stays quiet but holds his hand on his holstered gun.

The dispatcher says that she'll see what she can do and hangs up the phone. Afraid of getting shot, the OCer doesn't try to call his lawyer as he wishes to, but he is happy knowing that he is recording the cop with audio and video and should be able to call his lawyer soon.

Very shortly thereafter, two more officers arrive. The first responding officer tells them that the OCer called 911 and asked for the MSP to come to the scene.

The OCer is belittled and called expletives by the backup officers. Among other things, the cops say, "What the f*** makes you think you can just carry a gun like that?" and "If you're gonna be an a**hole and carry a gun for everyone to see, you can expect this every time!"

The OCer is told to put his hands on the first responding officer's push bumper, and he is then disarmed and patted down, and his wallet is taken from him. His ID and CPL are run through the LEIN system, despite the fact he refused consent. They take his phone from him as well as his audio recorder, which they shut off. They also take his hat off, but they remain completely oblivious to the fact that it is a video camera, which is still recording. **The OCer stays quiet and doesn't say a word.**

The cops tell the OCer he may relax and that they are sure he isn't dangerous now that he is disarmed. The lesser-ranking backup cop lectures him with lies about how stupid he is being and how they can charge him with a slew of crimes and take his CPL away. Meanwhile, the other two cops talk in a squad car. **The OCer doesn't say a single word; he hasn't said a thing since he talked to the 911 dispatcher.**

After several minutes, the first responding officer gets out of the car and hands the OCer back his property, saying "I'm sorry for the confusion, you're good to go." He turns around and walks back toward his car. He is concerned because he just called the prosecutor, who informed him that he is an idiot who is now liable to get sued, especially since the entire department is on record as knowing that OC is legal from a training course they completed.

The OCer asks the officers for their name and badge numbers, but they refuse and leave. No matter, he thinks to himself, since he has them on video and can FOIA their reports and all the video and audio they took as well.

The police promptly leave, and the OCer turns his audio recorder back on in case of any more trouble. His hat is still running. He then calls his lawyer on his way home.

Following advice from his lawyer, the OCer uploads and saves the evidence to his computer and then saves it on two disks and a USB drive. He contacts the MSP with a complaint of unlawful LEIN system access, which they later investigate but take no punitive actions on.

He submits a carefully written FOIA request to the PD for all evidence, including all of their video, audio, written or typed reports and the 911 call.

Unable to afford the lawsuit he wishes to bring upon the department, he types out a color of law complaint, has some other legally savvy OCDO members proofread it and submits it to the FBI.

Finally, he uploads his video and audio and puts them on youtube. He also scans copies of the police reports he received copies of and posts them on www.opencarry.org.

The police department is now publicly embarrassed and well aware of how badly they can be hit with a lawsuit. The FBI then contacts the PD. The PD comes up with a dishonest but effective means to weasel their way out of the Federal charges that the FBI could have pressed. The FBI tells them that it better not happen again.

The OCer is disgusted and shaken up, but he continues OCing.

The important lesson to be taken from this story is to NEVER talk to the police when they are detaining you. You may want to ask if you are being detained, but many times even this isn't necessary because it is often obvious when you are being detained.

If the police confirm that you aren't being detained, say nothing else and walk away immediately. If they say that you are being detained, or give you a confusing response that might indicate you are being detained, call 911 if possible; otherwise, just say nothing, and record away.

The only other words worth saying to the police are "I don't consent to any searches!" However, saying nothing is the same thing as denying consent. If the police can cite a reasonable, articulateable suspicion to detain you, it does not matter whether you deny consent, as they can legally search you with or without consent. But OCing is legal and not reasonable suspicion for a Terry stop according to JL v Florida (Exhibit 2 D), and so it is nearly impossible that officers will have a reason to detain you that will later hold up in court. However, police are very good at intimidating people into giving consent, which can fool you into throwing away your rights if you fall for it. This is why staying quiet and avoiding even a single extra word are so important.

To reinforce the importance of not talking to the police, you may want to look up a video online entitled "Don't talk to police." It is a video of a lecture by a former defense attorney and current law professor on why you should never ever talk to police, particularly if they are investigating you.

Another crucially important lesson from this OC story is the role of covert recording devices. Police often take easily identifiable recorders during a stop, and so it is imperative that they do not know how many recording devices are being used to record them.

Some cell phones can also be used as recorders, but police officers know this. So, do not trust a cell phone for use as a covert recording system, even if you have a clever covert recorder application downloaded. It will do no good with your phone turned off or with the battery pulled out. However, it's a great option to have as another backup device.

It should be clear now how to effectively handle police encounters. But in order to best understand the importance of your behavior during police encounters, read the following story. It is another compilation of true stories that is similar to the first story, except that this time it is full of mistakes by the OCer.

A non-CPL holding OCer is walking down the street.

He sees a police car approaching him. His heart starts pounding like it does for most people in this situation, and he isn't sure what to do.

The cop stops his car right beside the OCer and gets out of the car with one hand on his gun, which isn't drawn. He screams at the OCer to put his hands up, which the OCer does.

The cop tells him, "No one's going to get hurt, just stay right like that and keep your mouth shut. My supervisor will be here shortly."

After several minutes, his supervisor, a Lieutenant, arrives.

The Lieutenant asks the OCer, "You don't have any warrants, right? So you don't mind if we check?"

The OCer is both scared and offended. He states that he is not a felon – "go right ahead and check." **He thus gives away any Constitutional rights to privacy, legalizing an otherwise unlawful detention.**

After he disarms and pats down the OCer, the Lieutenant begins questioning the OCer, and the OCer, too scared and uneducated to know any better, answers the questions.

The Lieutenant and the first responding officer go through a good cop-bad cop routine, with the goal of making the OCer want to "calm them down" by talking. In reality, this is an extremely common manipulative technique used by the police to get the uneducated public to run their mouths and confess to acts that they may not even know are illegal.

As part of the routine, the officers repeat the same questions about 10 times, each time asking in different ways and putting varying amounts of stress on the OCer. This could have all been avoided if the OCer had simply stayed quiet in the first place.
Through their intimidation and bullying, the police find out that the OCer was on his way back from a liquor store, where he bought a

pop. Thus, the OCer admitted to committing a crime, since the store has a liquor license. They also find out that he is parked at a church and didn't have permission of the owners of the church to be there.

As a result, the OCer is charged with a felony. He spends thousands of dollars getting some of the best legal council available. He manages to plead down to a misdemeanor, ends up losing his right to own guns for several years and has to shovel horse manure every weekend at a County Sheriff's horse stable for six months.

Everything in this story has happened! Don't let any of it happen to you!

A still frame picture of a FOIA'd video of OCDO member Hammaneggs being assaulted by a Warren PD officer.

Three of the more than one dozen East Lansing PD officers who detained OCDO members at Ponderosa in East Lansing in February 2010.

DRAFTING THE IDEAL FREEDOM OF INFORMATION ACT (FOIA) REQUEST

Many people are not aware that the state of Michigan requires most government entities to disclose all information that is not "extremely personal in nature" or classified for security reasons through Act 442 of 1976 (Exhibit 18 A). It is relatively easy to obtain this information. Or, better said, it is relatively easy to *try* to obtain this information, since many PDs will illegally short-change you when you make such requests.

It is important to submit a FOIA immediately after an incident. This request should be done in the form of a very professional memorandum that says only what needs to be said and little to nothing else. Complaints and most other details are irrelevant to your information request and best left out, no matter how angry you may be.

Below is an example of a generic but well-formatted FOIA memo. It was originally drafted by Attorney Dean Greenblatt (see page 45 for his contact information) for OCDO member TheSzerdi. TheSzerdi later edited it to make it a generic, all-purpose FOIA sample.

March X, 20XX

VIA CERTIFIED MAIL
RETURN RECEIPT REQUESTED

FOIA COORDINATOR
ANYWHERE POLICE DEPARTMENT
1300 BLANK ST
POLICE HEADQUARTERS
ANYWHERE, MI 48484

RE: FOIA Request

Dear FOIA Coordinator:

On MONTH DATE, YEAR at approximately TIME, Anywhere Police Department Officers XXXXXXXXX and XXXXXXXXXXX engaged in the detention and investigation of a person with a pistol on the sidewalk at Some Street between That St and Another St in the City of Anywhere. As a result of Officers XXXXXX and XXXXX's investigation, Officer XXXXXX issued citations for firearm violations to You Yourself.

Pursuant to the Michigan Freedom of Information Act, MCL §15.231, I am requesting copies of documents relating to the aforementioned incident, including:

Any and all recordings of radio communications related in any way to the dispatch, response or request for assistance by the officers involved with the incident;

Any and all video recordings of the incident, including patrol car video;

Any and all documents that identify the officers dispatched

to the scene as a result of the incident, including the police report, roll call rosters, vehicle logs and audio recordings;

Any and all emails, memos, letters and/or other correspondence between employees of the Anywhere Police Department and any other person regarding the incident; and,

Any and all property booking notes, cards and papers recording the property seized by Officer XXXXXX and XXXXXXXXXXXX associated with the incident.

Should the cost for researching, compiling and copying the requested information exceed $30.00, please inform me of the anticipated cost and provide me with a time and place for a physical inspection of the requested information before researching, compiling or copying the requested information.

Please respond to this request by replying to the following address:

You Yourself
123 Anystreet
Whatever City, MI 48484
313-555-5555

I appreciate your anticipated cooperation with this request. If you have any questions, please do not hesitate to call me at the number above.

Sincerely,

You Yourself

REPORTING UNLAWFUL LEIN ACCESS

Many times when Michigan OCers have been illegally detained, their IDs have also been illegally seized and run through the Michigan Law Enforcement Information Network (LEIN) system. The LEIN system is regulated by MCL 28.214. (Exhibit 20 A).
It is the MSP's job to investigate wrongful uses of LEIN. Importantly, MCL 28.214 says:

Subsection (3) A person shall not access, use, or disclose nonpublic information governed under this act for personal use or gain.

In the opinion of the author, running a person's ID through this system without permission or without reasonable articulateable suspicion is a crime that infringes on the Fourth Amendment and other Federal laws. For this reason, unwarranted and non-consensual LEIN access should be reported to the MSP. The following information is straight from the MSP's web site at http://www.michigan.gov/msp/0,1607,7-123-1589_1878_8311-16246--,00.html.

LEIN and Criminal History Records - Inappropriate Access

To report inappropriate access to the Michigan State Police for LEIN & CHR record information, write, fax, or e-mail:
Capt. Charles Bush, Commander
Criminal Records Division
P.O. Box 30634
Lansing, MI 48913
bushce@michigan.gov
Fax: 517-241-0865

The following information is needed to investigate the inappropriate access (some of this information may be unknown):

1. *What record was accessed? Include the name, date of birth, driver license number, license plate number and details surrounding the potential misuse.*

2. *Why do you believe the information was obtained inappropriately?*

3. *When did the access in question take place (get as close to the day and time as possible - within a week or two is best)?*

4. *Where the access occurred (which State Police post, sheriff department, police department, court, etc.).*

5. *Who accessed the record?*

6. *Telephone number where you can be reached, if we have any questions.*

Upon receipt of the request to investigate a potential LEIN violation, the LEIN traffic will be reviewed and a determination made as to whether or not there is a need for further investigation. The investigation will take 60 - 90 days under normal circumstances. Upon closure of the case the person/agency reporting the possible LEIN violation will be notified in writing as to whether or not the case was founded or unfounded.

COLOR OF LAW COMPLAINTS TO THE FBI

A properly written color of law complaint is very long, so long that it isn't worthwhile to write one out here. In addition, each situation is unique, so one example may be very different from what you may need for your complaint. So, instead of providing a sample, the following is a basic overview that simply but effectively quotes the FBI's home page information on color of law complaints at: http://www.fbi.gov/hq/cid/civilrights/color.htm.

U.S. law enforcement officers and other officials like judges, prosecutors, and security guards have been given tremendous power by local, state, and federal government agencies—authority they must have to enforce the law and ensure justice in our country. These powers include the authority to detain and arrest suspects, to search and seize property, to bring criminal charges, to make rulings in court, and to use deadly force in certain situations.

Preventing abuse of this authority, however, is equally necessary to the health of our nation's democracy. That's why it's a federal crime for anyone acting under "color of law" willfully to deprive or conspire to deprive a person of a right protected by the Constitution or U.S. law. "Color of law" simply means that the person is using authority given to him or her by a local, state, or federal government agency.

The FBI is the lead federal agency for investigating color of law abuses, which include acts carried out by government officials operating both within and beyond the limits of their lawful authority. Off-duty conduct may be covered if the perpetrator asserted his or her official status in some way.

During Fiscal Year 2005, the FBI investigated more than 1,100 color of law cases. Most of these crimes fall into five broad areas:

- *excessive force;*
- *sexual assaults;*
- *false arrest and fabrication of evidence;*
- *deprivation of property; and*
- *failure to keep from harm.*

Excessive force: In making arrests, maintaining order, and defending life, law enforcement officers are allowed to use whatever force is "reasonably" necessary. The breadth and scope of the use of force is vast—from just the physical presence of the officer...to the use of deadly force. Violations of federal law occur when it can be shown that the force used was willfully "unreasonable" or "excessive."

Sexual assaults by officials acting under color of law can happen in jails, during traffic stops, or in other settings where officials might use their position of authority to coerce an individual into sexual compliance. The compliance is generally gained because of a threat of an official action against the person if he or she doesn't comply.

False arrest and fabrication of evidence: The Fourth Amendment of the U.S. Constitution guarantees the right against unreasonable searches or seizures. A law enforcement official using authority provided under the color of law is allowed to stop individuals and, under certain circumstances, to search them and retain their property. It is in the abuse of that discretionary power— such as an unlawful detention or illegal confiscation of property—that a violation of a person's civil rights may occur.

Fabricating evidence against or falsely arresting an individual also violates the color of law statute, taking away the person's rights of due process and unreasonable seizure. In the case of deprivation of property, the color of law statute would be violated by unlawfully obtaining or maintaining a person's property, which oversteps or misapplies the official's authority.

The Fourteenth Amendment secures the right to due process; the Eighth Amendment prohibits the use of cruel and unusual punishment. During an arrest or detention, these rights can be violated by the use of force amounting to punishment (summary judgment). The person accused of a crime must be allowed the opportunity to have a trial and should not be subjected to punishment without having been afforded the opportunity of the legal process.

Failure to keep from harm: The public counts on its law enforcement officials to protect local communities. If it's shown that an official willfully failed to keep an individual from harm, that official could be in violation of the color of law statute.

Filing a Complaint:

To file a color of law complaint, contact your <u>*local FBI*</u>

office by telephone, in writing, or in person. The following information should be provided:

• all identifying information for the victim(s);
• as much identifying information as possible for the subject(s), including position, rank, and
 agency employed;
• date and time of incident;
• location of incident;
• names, addresses, and telephone numbers of any witness(es);
• a complete chronology of events; and
• any report numbers and charges with respect to the incident.

You may also contact the United States Attorney's Office in your district or send a written complaint to:

Assistant Attorney General
Civil Rights Division
Criminal Section
950 Pennsylvania Avenue, Northwest
Washington, DC 20530

FBI investigations vary in length. Once our investigation is complete, we forward the findings to the U.S. Attorney's Office within the local jurisdiction and to the U.S. Department of Justice in Washington, D.C., which decide whether or not to proceed toward prosecution and handle any prosecutions that follow.

Civil Applications

Title 42, U.S.C., Section 14141 makes it unlawful for state or local law enforcement agencies to allow officers to engage in a pattern or practice of conduct that deprives persons of rights protected by the Constitution or U.S. laws. This law, commonly referred to as the Police Misconduct Statute, gives the Department of Justice authority to seek civil remedies in cases where law enforcement agencies have policies or practices that foster a pattern of misconduct by employees. This action is directed against an agency, not against individual officers. The types of issues which may initiate a pattern and practice investigation include:

• Lack of supervision/monitoring of officers' actions;

• Lack of justification or reporting by officers on incidents involving the use of force;
• Lack of, or improper training of, officers; and
• Citizen complaint processes that treat complainants as adversaries.

Under Title 42, U.S.C., Section 1997, the Department of Justice has the ability to initiate civil actions against mental hospitals, retardation facilities, jails, prisons, nursing homes, and juvenile detention facilities when there are allegations of systemic derivations of the constitutional rights of institutionalized persons.

If you ever find yourself needing to write a color of law complaint, it would be wise to seek the help of legally savvy Michigan members of OCDO. Some members have made this type of complaint before and would be very happy to help. In addition, you should know that the FBI is a very straight-forward agency; they will ask you questions if they need clarification and will not mind if you need to ask them questions.

PISTOL CARRYING LEGAL QUIZ

Answers appear on page 174.

(1)- In which of the following places can a non-CPL holder generally open carry?
A- A moving car.
B- A Marathon gas station that sells beer but NOT hard liquor.
C- A coffee shop.
D- A church.

(2)- Where may a CPL holder open carry?
A- A court house.
B- National parks.
C- A post office.
D- All of the above are generally illegal.
E- Carry at any of the above is preemptively allowed by Michigan state law (concealed or otherwise) if you have a CPL.

(3)- Which of the following is widely accepted as open carrying according to state law, AG opinion and the opinion of most open carriers in Michigan?
A- A Serpa paddle holster with a t-shirt tucked over part of the grip.
B- A flap holster that almost covers the entire gun.
C- A Bianchi IWB holster.
D- A drop-leg holster.
E- A and D only.

(4)- An OCer enjoys riding motorcycles and bicycles.

She has no CPL. May she open carry on either?

A-It appears to be legal, but the law isn't as clear as it should be, so she risks being criminally charged if she does. This is not advised as of this writing.

B- By Michigan law, a gun becomes magically concealed as soon as you mount a bicycle or motorcycle, and therefore, she must have a CPL to OC on her bikes.

C- Only an idiot could think that an openly holstered pistol is concealed if it's worn by a cyclist, which is why open carry on bikes of all types is preemptively legal by state law.

(5)- Which of the following is a legal action while in possession of a firearm on school property?

A- An 18-year-old high school senior leaving his trigger-locked, cased and unloaded shotgun in his trunk so he can go hunt deer after school gets out.

B- A CPL holder carrying concealed and driving his car as he drops his daughter off at elementary school.

C- A non-CPL holder open carrying on a Sunday afternoon while sitting on a bench in front of a middle school.

D- A CPL holder open carrying to a school football game.

E- B and D only.

(6)- Which of the following could constitute brandishing?

A- Wearing camouflage face paint and black clothing and walking through a crowded park with an AK in your hands.

B- Wearing a 44 magnum in a drop-leg holster.

C- Parking in a state park parking lot full of mountain bikers and taking your 12 gauge out and loading it to hunt rabbits, terrifying several mountain bikers.
D- A and B only

(7)-Which MUST exist for deadly force to be justified?
A- A reasonable fear of imminent death.
B- A reasonable fear of imminent serious bodily injury.
C- A reasonable fear of imminent forced sexual penetration.
D- Any or all of the above.

(8)- In which of the following examples are you required to show an officer your ID and/or CPL?
A- When an officer sees you open carrying and finds it suspicious.
B- When you are witnessed open carrying, a 911 call is made, and the police say that you have to show ID because the call is reasonable suspicion.
C- When an officer sees you and stops you while you're open carrying in a liquor-licensed establishment.
D- Whenever asked if you have a driver's license, because of implied consent.
E- None of the above.

(9)- Which of the following are locations that are illegal for a CPL holder to open carry in?
A- The state Capitol building, police stations and City Hall.
B- K-12 Schools, state-run colleges and any vocational training schools.
C- Restaurants that serve alcohol for onsite consumption, bars and taverns.

D- Banks, credit unions, theaters and sports arenas.
E- None of the above. Having a CPL in Michigan gives you more rights to carry than almost any other state in the country.

(10)- Several OCers are talking about carrying to movie theaters. Who is right?
A- OCer A says that you can open carry at a theater without a CPL, but you must be careful about where you park because of transportation rules.
B- OCer B says that you can open carry to a theater with or without a CPL because no alcohol is sold there.
C- OCer C says that open carry is fine, but you must have a CPL.
D- Only A and C are correct.

(11)- A CPL holder wants to carry a loaded shotgun in the front seat of his car. Does Michigan allow this?
A- This is legal with a CPL, but only if it's unloaded in the barrel and magazine.
B- Yes, but it must be defined as a pistol by Michigan law with an overall length of 26-30", and it must be registered as a pistol as well.
C- Michigan law ONLY allows pistols in the passenger compartment of a car and bans sawed-off shotguns, which are the only shotguns with pistol dimensions, and so shotguns in the passenger compartment are illegal.
D- Long guns over 30" can be stored within reach of the passengers of a car, but they must be unloaded and encased.

(12)- Which of the following is true about Michigan state land and state parks?

A- You may only carry a loaded firearm in a state park if you are hunting or possess a CPL while carrying a pistol. In all other situations, firearms must be unloaded in the barrel and magazine.

B- Any safe backstop on state land may be used for target shooting only during daylight hours and never during bow season.

C- Some state parks have shooting ranges where you have to pay, while others are free.

D- A and C only

(13)- At an OCDO meeting, four open carriers are discussing carrying in banks. Who is right?

A- OCer A says that according to Michigan law, you can OC or CC at a bank, but you must have a CPL.

B- OCer B says that because most banks are controlled by the Federal government, carry by anyone other than sworn Federal officers is prohibited in most circumstances.

C- OCer C says that Michigan law does not statutorily prohibit carrying at financial institutions, so anyone may open carry there, but you could alarm bank employees and have the police called.

D- OCer D says that you should always avoid open carrying in banks because people will think you could be a robber, and the police might shoot you.

(14)- Which of the following is protected and ensured by the Bill Of Rights?

A- You have a right to remain silent to avoid self incrimination.

B- It's a Constitutional obligation of able-bodied adults to be armed to protect the security of their free states.

C- Without probable cause, no government agent has a right to search or seize property. This includes demanding ID for merely participating in the obligation mentioned in B.

D- All of the above are true.

(15)- A pastor wants to carry his pistol to his church and encourage everyone who attends to do the same if they own pistols.

A- He can't carry, nor can any members of his church, because Michigan law forbids carry at churches.

B- As the owner of the church property, he has the right to supersede state law and allow OC by non-CPL holders and CC or OC by those with CPLs.

C- Because wine is served on some Sundays, the Michigan Liquor Control Act comes into play, and therefore, it is illegal for anyone other than police who are not drinking to possess firearms in the church.

D- A and C only

(16)- A group of OCers are discussing the gun shows that used to take place at the Pontiac Silverdome. Who is correct?

A- OCer A says that it was a bad place to host the shows because it's illegal to carry there at all, as sports arenas are gun-free zones.

B- OCer B says that the owner of the Silverdome was able to bypass state law by giving his specific permission to possess firearms there.

C- OCer C says that you can open carry in any of the gun free zones as long as you have a CPL, and so the Silverdome would have had no authority to kick anyone out.

D- OCer D says that private property owners have the right to kick anyone out whenever they please, so if the Silverdome said no loaded firearms, you could get charged with trespassing if you disobeyed the request.
E- B and D only

(17)- Several OCers are talking about liquor-licensed businesses and where they can carry. Who is correct?
A- OCer A says that you can't carry at a bar even if you do have a CPL because bars are gun-free zones.
B- OCer B says that anyone, whether they have a CPL or not, can open carry at a liquor-licensed business, as long as they make less than 50% of their income from alcohol sales.
C- OCer C says that the you can't carry at ANY liquor-licensed business if you don't have a CPL, and if you do have a CPL, you must open carry if they make 50% or more of their income from alcohol sold for on-site consumption.
D- OCer D says that if you're going to have even a small amount of alcohol, your gun should be locked in the trunk, with the ammunition stored separately from the firearm.
E- C and D only.

(18)- Preemption in Michigan nullifies which of the following types of regulations?
A- City ordinances.
B- Federal laws that unjustly regulate inner-state activities.
C- City and state laws regarding knives and pepper spray, but only if you've got a CCW.
D- State and city laws against transporting loaded long

guns in the passenger compartment of a vehicle, but only for CPL holders.

(19)- An OCer has a NFA-registered Mac 11, but he has no CPL. May he open carry it?
A- Federal law specifically prohibits transportation or possession of NFA weapons unless at or on the way to work, home, a place of repair or a shooting range. But there is an exemption for CPL holders.
B- Michigan law considers it a pistol, and assuming all Federal laws are complied with, he may carry it under the restrictions of Michigan laws concerning pistols.
C- Because Federal Firearms Licenses are required to own machine guns, he doesn't need to worry because his FFL supersedes state law, and he may carry it almost anywhere he chooses to, concealed or openly.
D- A and B only

RECCOMENDED SHOOTING INSTRUCTORS AND LAWYERS

PLEASE NOTE THAT WHILE THESE INSTRUCTORS AND LAWYERS ARE LISTED WITH THEIR PERMISSION, NONE HAVE ENDORSED THIS BOOK. THIS BOOK IS NOT A REFLECTION OF THEIR OPINIONS.

--Firearms Instructors--
Wild West Academy of SE Michigan
>   CPL instruction, and unarmed self defense.
>   Visit online at www.wildwestacademy.com
>   Contact at wildwestacademy@aol.com or call
>   **248-506-3472**

Jan Jay
>   CPL instruction, Monroe County
>   Contact at **734-657-3268**

Rick Ector
>   Detroitccw.com
>   info@detroitccw.com
>   313-733-7404

--Lawyers Specializing in Firearms Law--
Dean Greenblatt
>   Attorney specializing in firearms and aviation
>   4190 Telegraph Road
>   Suite 3500
>   Bloomfield Hills, Mi, 48308
>   248-644-7520

CHAPTER 13

LAW, CASE LAW AND AG OPINION GUIDE

APPENDIX A: STATE LAWS

Michigan's Constitution: Article 1, Section 6 of
Michigan's Constitution: Every person has the right to
bear arms for defense of himself and the state.

EXHIBIT 1 A PREEMPTION
MCL 123.1101 Definitions.

Sec. 1.

As used in this act:

(a) "Local unit of government" means a city, village,
township, or county.

(b) "Pistol" means that term as defined in section 222 of
the Michigan penal code, Act No. 328 of the Public
Acts of 1931, being section 750.222 of the Michigan
Compiled Laws.

123.1102 Regulation of pistols or other firearms.

Sec. 2.

A local unit of government shall not impose special
taxation on, enact or enforce any ordinance or
regulation pertaining to, or regulate in any other manner
the ownership, registration, purchase, sale, transfer,
transportation, or possession of pistols or other firearms,
ammunition for pistols or other firearms, or components

of pistols or other firearms, except as otherwise provided by federal law or a law of this state.

123.1103 Permissible prohibitions or regulation.

Sec. 3.

This act does not prohibit a local unit of government from doing either of the following:

(a) Prohibiting or regulating conduct with a pistol or other firearm that is a criminal offense under state law.

(b) Prohibiting or regulating the transportation, carrying, or possession of pistols and other firearms by employees of that local unit of government in the course of their employment with that local unit of government.

123.1104 Prohibiting discharge of pistol or other firearm.

Sec. 4.

This act does not prohibit a city or a charter township from prohibiting the discharge of a pistol or other firearm within the jurisdiction of that city or charter township.

EXHIBIT 2 A WEAPON DEFINITIONS

MCL 750.222 Definitions.

Sec. 222.

As used in this chapter:

(a) "Alcoholic liquor" means that term as defined in section 105 of the Michigan liquor control code of 1998, 1998 PA 58, MCL 436.1105.

(b) "Barrel length" means the internal length of a firearm as measured from the face of the closed breech of the firearm when it is unloaded, to the forward face of the end of the barrel.

(c) "Controlled substance" means a controlled substance or controlled substance analogue as those terms are defined in section 7104 of the public health code, 1978 PA 368, MCL 333.7104.

(d) "Firearm" means a weapon from which a dangerous projectile may be propelled by an explosive, or by gas or air. Firearm does not include a smooth bore rifle or handgun designed and manufactured exclusively for propelling by a spring, or by gas or air, BB's not exceeding .177 caliber.

(e) "Pistol" means a loaded or unloaded firearm that is 30 inches or less in length, or a loaded or unloaded firearm that by its construction and appearance conceals itself as a firearm.

(f) "Purchaser" means a person who receives a pistol from another person by purchase, gift, or loan.

(g) "Seller" means a person who sells, furnishes, loans, or gives a pistol to another person.

(h) "Shotgun" means a firearm designed or redesigned, made or remade, and intended to be fired from the shoulder and designed or redesigned and made or remade to use the energy of the explosive in a fixed shotgun shell to fire through a smooth bore either a number of ball shot or a single projectile for each single function of the trigger.

(i) "Short-barreled shotgun" means a shotgun having 1 or more barrels less than 18 inches in length or a weapon made from a shotgun, whether by alteration, modification, or otherwise, if the weapon as modified has an overall length of less than 26 inches.

(j) "Rifle" means a firearm designed or redesigned, made or remade, and intended to be fired from the shoulder and designed or redesigned and made or remade to use the energy of the explosive in a fixed metallic cartridge to fire only a single projectile through a rifled bore for each single pull of the trigger.

(k) "Short-barreled rifle" means a rifle having 1 or more barrels less than 16 inches in length or a weapon made from a rifle, whether by alteration, modification, or otherwise, if the weapon as modified has an overall length of less than 26 inches.

EXHIBIT 3 A PROHIBITED PLACES TO CARRY WITH NO CPL
MCL 750.234d Possession of firearm on certain premises prohibited; applicability; violation as misdemeanor; penalty.
Sec. 234d.
(1) Except as provided in subsection (2), a person shall not possess a firearm on the premises of any of the following:

(a) A depository financial institution or a subsidiary or affiliate of a depository financial institution.

(b) A church or other house of religious worship.

(c) A court.

(d) A theatre.

(e) A sports arena.

(f) A day care center.

(g) A hospital.

(h) An establishment licensed under the Michigan liquor control act, Act No. 8 of the Public Acts of the Extra Session of 1933, being sections 436.1 to 436.58 of the Michigan Compiled Laws.

(2) This section does not apply to any of the following:

(a) A person who owns, or is employed by or contracted by, an entity described in subsection (1) if the possession of that firearm is to provide security services for that entity.

(b) A peace officer.

(c) A person licensed by this state or another state to carry a concealed weapon.

(d) A person who possesses a firearm on the premises of an entity described in subsection (1) if that possession is with the permission of the owner or an agent of the owner of that entity.

(3) A person who violates this section is guilty of a misdemeanor punishable by imprisonment for not more

than 90 days or a fine of not more than $100.00, or both.

EXHIBIT 4 A NO CARRY AT K-12 SCHOOL WITHOUT CPL
MCL 750.237a Individuals engaging in proscribed conduct; violation; penalties; definitions.

Sec. 237a.

(1) An individual who engages in conduct proscribed under section 224, 224a, 224b, 224c, 224e, 226, 227, 227a, 227f, 234a, 234b, or 234c, or who engages in conduct proscribed under section 223(2) for a second or subsequent time, in a weapon free school zone is guilty of a felony punishable by 1 or more of the following:

(a)Imprisonment for not more than the maximum term of imprisonment authorized for the section violated.

(b)Community service for not more than 150 hours.

(c)A fine of not more than 3 times the maximum fine authorized for the section violated.

(2) An individual who engages in conduct proscribed under section 223(1), 224d, 226a, 227c, 227d, 231c, 232a(1) or (4), 233, 234, 234e, 234f, 235, 236, or 237, or who engages in conduct proscribed under section 223(2) for the first time, in a weapon free school zone is guilty of a misdemeanor punishable by 1 or more of the following:

(d)Imprisonment for not more than the maximum term of imprisonment authorized for the section violated or 93 days, whichever is greater.

(e)Community service for not more than 100 hours.

(f)A fine of not more than $2,000.00 or the maximum fine authorized for the section violated, whichever is greater.

(3) Subsections (1) and (2) do not apply to conduct proscribed under a section enumerated in those subsections to the extent that the proscribed conduct is otherwise exempted or authorized under this chapter.

(4) Except as provided in subsection (5), an individual who possesses a weapon in a weapon free school zone is guilty of a misdemeanor punishable by 1 or more of the following:

(g)Imprisonment for not more than 93 days.

(h)Community service for not more than 100 hours.

(i)A fine of not more than $2,000.00.

(5) Subsection (4) does not apply to any of the following:

(j)An individual employed by or contracted by a school if the possession of that weapon is to provide security services for the school.

(k)A peace officer.

(l)An individual licensed by this state or another state to carry a concealed weapon.

(m)An individual who possesses a weapon provided by a school or a school's instructor on school property for purposes of providing or receiving instruction in the use of that weapon.

(n)An individual who possesses a firearm on school property if that possession is with the permission of the school's principal or an agent of the school designated by the school's principal or the school board.

(o)An individual who is 18 years of age or older who is not a student at the school and who possesses a firearm on school property while transporting a student to or from the school if any of the following apply:

(h) The individual is carrying an antique firearm, completely unloaded, in a wrapper or container in the trunk of a vehicle while en route to or from a hunting or target shooting area or function involving the exhibition, demonstration or sale of antique firearms.

(i) (ii) The individual is carrying a firearm unloaded in a wrapper or container in the trunk of the person's vehicle, while in possession of a valid Michigan hunting license or proof of valid membership in an organization having shooting range facilities, and while en route to or from a hunting or target shooting area.

(j) (iii) The person is carrying a firearm unloaded in a wrapper or container in the trunk of the person's vehicle from the place of purchase to his or her home or place of business or to a place of repair or back to his or her home or place of business, or in moving goods from one place of abode or business to another place of abode or business.

(k) (iv) The person is carrying an unloaded firearm in the passenger compartment of a vehicle that does not have a trunk, if the person is otherwise complying with the requirements of subparagraph (ii) or (iii) and the wrapper or container is not readily accessible to the occupants of the vehicle.

(6) As used in this section:

(p)"Antique firearm" means either of the following:

(i)A firearm not designed or redesigned for using rimfire or conventional center fire ignition with fixed ammunition and manufactured in or before 1898, including a matchlock, flintlock, percussion cap, or similar type of ignition system or a replica of such a firearm, whether actually manufactured before or after the year 1898.

(ii)A firearm using fixed ammunition manufactured in or before 1898, for which ammunition is no longer manufactured in the United States and is not readily available in the ordinary channels of commercial trade.

(q)"School" means a public, private, denominational, or parochial school offering developmental kindergarten, kindergarten, or any grade from 1 through 12.

(r)"School property" means a building, playing field, or property used for school purposes to impart instruction to children or used for functions and events sponsored by a school, except a building used primarily for adult education or college extension courses.

(s)"Weapon free school zone" means school property and a vehicle used by a school to transport students to or from school property.

EXHIBIT 5 A REGISTRATION PROCESS "LICENSE TO CARRY"
MCL 28.422 License to purchase, carry, possess, or transport pistol; issuance; qualifications; applications; sale of pistol; exemptions; nonresidents; basic pistol safety brochure; forging application; implementation during business hours.
Sec. 2. **(1) Except as otherwise provided in this**

section, a person shall not purchase, carry, possess, or transport a pistol in this state without first having obtained a license for the pistol as prescribed in this section.

(2) A person who brings a pistol into this state who is on leave from active duty with the armed forces of the United States or who has been discharged from active duty with the armed forces of the United States shall obtain a license for the pistol within 30 days after his or her arrival in this state.

(3) The commissioner or chief of police of a city, township, or village police department that issues licenses to purchase, carry, possess, or transport pistols, or his or her duly authorized deputy, or the sheriff or his or her duly authorized deputy, in the parts of a county not included within a city, township, or village having an organized police department, in discharging the duty to issue licenses shall with due speed and diligence issue licenses to purchase, carry, possess, or transport pistols to qualified applicants residing within the city, village, township, or county, as applicable unless he or she has probable cause to believe that the applicant would be a threat to himself or herself or to other individuals, or would commit an offense with the pistol that would violate a law of this or another state or of the United States. An applicant is qualified if all of the following circumstances exist:

(a) The person is not subject to an order or disposition for which he or she has received notice and an opportunity for a hearing, and which was entered into the law enforcement information network pursuant to any of the following:

(i) Section 464a(1) of the mental health code, 1974 PA

258, MCL 330.1464a.

(ii) Section 5107 of the estates and protected individuals code, 1998 PA 386, MCL 700.5107, or section 444a of former 1978 PA 642.

(iii) Section 2950(10) of the revised judicature act of 1961, 1961 PA 236, MCL 600.2950.

(iv) Section 2950a(7) of the revised judicature act of 1961, 1961 PA 236, MCL 600.2950a.

(v) Section 14 of 1846 RS 84, MCL 552.14.

(vi) Section 6b(5) of chapter V of the code of criminal procedure, 1927 PA 175, MCL 765.6b, if the order has a condition imposed under section 6b(3) of chapter V of the code of criminal procedure, 1927 PA 175, MCL 765.6b.

(vii) Section 16b(1) of chapter IX of the code of criminal procedure, 1927 PA 175, MCL 769.16b.

(b) The person is 18 years of age or older or, if the seller is licensed under 18 USC 923, is 21 years of age or older.

(8) An individual who is not a resident of this state is not required to obtain a license under this section if all of the following conditions apply:

(a) The individual is licensed in his or her state of residence to purchase, carry, or transport a pistol.

(b) The individual is in possession of the license described in subdivision (a).

(c) The individual is the owner of the pistol he or she possesses, carries, or transports.

(d) The individual possesses the pistol for a lawful purpose as that term is defined in section 231a of the Michigan penal code, 1931 PA 328, MCL 750.231a.

(e) The individual is in this state for a period of 180 days or less and does not intend to establish residency in this state.

(9) An individual who is a nonresident of this state shall present the license described in subsection (8)(a) upon the demand of a police officer. An individual who violates this subsection is guilty of a misdemeanor punishable by imprisonment for not more than 90 days or a fine of not more than $100.00, or both.

(10) The licensing authority may require a person claiming active duty status with the United States armed forces to provide proof of 1 or both of the following:

(a) The person's home of record.

(b) Permanent active duty assignment in this state.

(11) This section does not apply to a person who is younger than the age required under subsection (3)(b) and who possesses a pistol if all of the following conditions apply:

(a) The person is not otherwise prohibited from possessing that pistol.

(b) The person is at a recognized target range.

(c) The person possesses the pistol for the purpose of target practice or instruction in the safe use of a pistol.

(d) The person's parent or guardian is physically present and supervising the person.

(e) The owner of the pistol is physically present.

(12) This section does not apply to a person who possesses a pistol if all of the following conditions apply:

(a) The person is not otherwise prohibited from possessing a pistol.

(b) The person is at a recognized target range or shooting facility.

(c) The person possesses the pistol for the purpose of target practice or instruction in the safe use of a pistol.

(d) The owner of the pistol is physically present and supervising the use of the pistol.

(13) The licensing authority shall provide a basic pistol safety brochure to each applicant for a license under this section before the applicant answers the basic pistol safety review questionnaire. A basic pistol safety brochure shall contain, but is not limited to providing, information on all of the following subjects:

(a) Rules for safe handling and use of pistols.

(b) Safe storage of pistols.

(c) Nomenclature and description of various types of pistols.

(d) The responsibilities of owning a pistol.

(14) The basic pistol safety brochure shall be supplied in addition to the safety pamphlet required by section 9b.

(15) The basic pistol safety brochure required in subsection (13) shall be produced by a national nonprofit membership organization that provides voluntary pistol safety programs that include training individuals in the safe handling and use of pistols.

(16) A person who forges any matter on an application for a license under this section is guilty of a felony, punishable by imprisonment for not more than 4 years

or a fine of not more than $2,000.00, or both.

(17) A licensing authority shall implement this section during all of the licensing authority's normal business hours and shall set hours for implementation that allow an applicant to use the license within the time period set forth in subsection (4).

EXHIBIT 6 A ACT 75 OF 2006

AN ACT to amend 1927 PA 372, entitled "An act to regulate and license the selling, purchasing, possessing, and carrying of certain firearms and gas ejecting devices; to prohibit the buying, selling, or carrying of certain firearms and gas ejecting devices without a license or other authorization; to provide for the forfeiture of firearms under certain circumstances; to provide for penalties and remedies; to provide immunity from civil liability under certain circumstances; to prescribe the powers and duties of certain state and local agencies; to prohibit certain conduct against individuals who apply for or receive a license to carry a concealed pistol; to make appropriations; to prescribe certain conditions for the appropriations; and to repeal all acts and parts of acts inconsistent with this act," by amending section12

(MCL 28.432), as amended by 2004 PA 99.

The People of the State of Michigan enact:

Sec. 12. (1) Sections 2 and 9 do not apply to any of the following:

(a) A police or correctional agency of the United States or of this state or any subdivision of this state.

(b) The United States army, air force, navy, or marine corps.

(c) An organization authorized by law to purchase or receive weapons from the United States or from this state.

(d) The national guard, armed forces reserves, or other duly authorized military organization.

(e) A member of an entity or organization described in subdivisions (a) to (d) for a pistol while engaged in the course of his or her duties with that entity or while going to or returning from those duties.

(f) A United States citizen holding a license to carry a pistol concealed upon his or her person issued by another state.

(g) The regular and ordinary transportation of a pistol as merchandise by an authorized agent of a person licensed to manufacture firearms or a licensed dealer.

(h) Purchasing, owning, carrying, possessing, using, or transporting an antique firearm. As used in this subdivision, "antique firearm" means that term as defined in section 231a of the Michigan penal code, 1931 PA 328, MCL 750.231a.

(i) An individual carrying, possessing, using, or transporting a pistol belonging to another individual, if the other individual's pistol is properly licensed and inspected under this act and the individual carrying, possessing, using, or transporting the pistol has obtained a license under section 5b to carry a concealed pistol.

(2) The amendatory act that added subdivision (h) shall be known and may be cited as the "Janet Kukuk act".

Enacting section 1. This amendatory act takes effect July 1, 2006.

This act is ordered to take immediate effect.

EXHIBIT 7 A EXCEPTIONS TO MCL 750.227(2) MCL 750.231a Exceptions to MCL 750.227(2); definitions.

Sec. 231a.

(1) Subsection (2) of section 227 does not apply to any of the following:

(a) To a person holding a valid license to carry a pistol concealed upon his or her person issued by his or her state of residence except where the pistol is carried in nonconformance with a restriction appearing on the license.

(b) To the regular and ordinary transportation of pistols as merchandise by an authorized agent of a person licensed to manufacture firearms.

(c) To a person carrying an antique firearm as defined in subsection (2), completely unloaded in a closed case or container designed for the storage of firearms in the trunk of a vehicle.

(d) To a person while transporting a pistol for a lawful purpose that is licensed by the owner or occupant of the motor vehicle in compliance with section 2 of 1927 PA 372, MCL 28.422, and the pistol is unloaded in a closed case designed for the storage of firearms in the trunk of the vehicle.

(e) To a person while transporting a pistol for a lawful purpose that is licensed by the owner or occupant of the motor vehicle in compliance with section 2 of 1927 PA 372, MCL 28.422, and the pistol is unloaded in a closed case designed for the storage of firearms in a vehicle that does not have a trunk and is not readily accessible to the occupants of the vehicle.

(2) As used in this section:

(a) "Antique firearm" means either of the following:

(i) A firearm not designed or redesigned for using rimfire or conventional center fire ignition with fixed ammunition and manufactured in or before 1898, including a matchlock, flintlock, percussion cap, or similar type of ignition system or replica of such a firearm, whether actually manufactured before or after 1898.

(ii) A firearm using fixed ammunition manufactured in or before 1898, for which ammunition is no longer manufactured in the United States and is not readily available in the ordinary channels of commercial trade.

(b) "Lawful purpose" includes the following:

(i) While en route to or from a hunting or target shooting area.

(ii) While transporting a pistol en route to or from his or her home or place of business and place of repair.

(iii) While moving goods from 1 place of abode or business to another place of abode or business.

(iv) While transporting a licensed pistol en route to or from a law enforcement agency or for the purpose of having a law enforcement official take possession of the weapon.

(v) While en route to or from his or her abode or place

of business and a gun show or places of purchase or sale.

(vi) While en route to or from his or her abode to a public shooting facility or public land where discharge of firearms is permitted by law, rule, regulation, or local ordinance.

(vii) While en route to or from his or her abode to a private property location where the pistol is to be used as is permitted by law, rule, regulation, or local ordinance.

EXHIBIT 8 A NO WEAPONS IN CASINOS
R 432.1212 Weapons in casino.

Rule 212. (1) An individual may not carry a firearm or other weapon in a casino, except for the following entities:

(a) State, county, city, township, or village law enforcement officers, as defined in section 2(e) of Act No. 203 of the Public Acts of 1965, as amended, being § 28.601 et seq. of the Michigan Compiled Laws.

(b) Federal law enforcement officers, as defined in 5 U.S.C. § 8331.

(c) Armored car personnel picking up or delivering currency at secured areas.

(2) Law enforcement officers conducting official duties within a casino shall, to the extent practicable, advise the Michigan state police gaming section of their presence.

(3) Private casino security personnel may carry handcuffs while on duty in a casino

EXHIBIT 9 A COMMUNITY COLLEGES ACT

Community Colleges Act. Act 331 of 1966

MCL 389.125 Board of trustees; payment of claims against community college district; gifts; bylaws.
Sec. 125.
The board of trustees may:

(a) Certify to the treasurer of the community college district for payment out of the funds thereof all claims and demands against the board or community college district, which shall be allowed by the board under rules and regulations it may establish.

(b) Borrow money or other property and accept contributions, capital grants, gifts, donations, services or other financial assistance from the United States of America or any agency or instrumentality thereof.

(c) Accept by gift or devise private property. They may accept from any county, township or other governmental unit any contribution authorized by its governing body as provided in sections 791 to 795 of Act No. 269 of the Public Acts of 1955, as amended, being sections 340.791 to 340.795 of the Compiled Laws of 1948. They shall likewise be entitled to receive from the state all grants of state aid, in the same manner and proportion, as any other community college.

(d) Adopt bylaws, rules and regulations for its own government and for the control and government of the community college district.

(e) Acquire and hold in the name of the district all real property and improvements acquired and erected under the provisions of this act.

(f) To do all other things in its judgment necessary for the proper establishment, maintenance, management and carrying on of the community college.

<u>EXHIBIT 10 A</u> CONCEALED CARRY DISCLOSURE TO POLICE WHEN STOPPED MCL 28.425f Concealed pistol license; possession; disclosure to police officer; violation; penalty; seizure; forfeiture; "peace officer" defined.

Sec. 5f.

(1) An individual who is licensed under this act to carry a concealed pistol shall have his or her license to carry that pistol in his or her possession at all times he or she is carrying a concealed pistol.(2) An individual who is licensed under this act to carry a concealed pistol and who is carrying a concealed pistol shall show both of the following to a peace officer upon request by that peace officer:

(a) His or her license to carry a concealed pistol.

(b) His or her driver license or Michigan personal identification card.

(3) An individual licensed under this act to carry a concealed pistol and who is carrying a concealed pistol and who is stopped by a peace officer shall immediately disclose to the peace officer that he or she is carrying a pistol concealed upon his or her person or in his or her

vehicle.

(4) An individual who violates subsection (1) or (2) is responsible for a state civil infraction and may be fined not more than $100.00.

(5) An individual who violates subsection (3) is responsible for a state civil infraction and may be fined as follows:

(a) For a first offense, by a fine of not more than $500.00 or by the individual's license to carry a concealed pistol being suspended for 6 months,

or both.

(b) For a subsequent offense within 3 years of a prior offense, by a fine of not more than $1,000.00 and by the individual's license to carry a concealed pistol being revoked.

(6) If an individual is found responsible for a state civil infraction under this section, the court shall notify the department of state police and the concealed weapon licensing board that issued the license of that determination.

(7) A pistol carried in violation of this section is subject to immediate seizure by a peace officer. If a peace officer seizes a pistol under this subsection, the individual has 45 days in which to display his or her license or documentation to an authorized employee of the law enforcement entity that employs the peace officer. If the individual displays his or her license or documentation to an authorized employee of the law enforcement entity that employs the peace officer within the 45-day period, the authorized employee of that law enforcement entity shall return the pistol to the

individual unless the individual is prohibited by law from possessing a firearm. If the individual does not display his or her license or documentation within the 45-day period, the pistol is subject to forfeiture as provided in section 5g. A pistol is not subject to immediate seizure under this subsection if both of the following circumstances exist:

(a) The individual has his or her driver license or Michigan personal identification card in his or her possession when the violation occurs.

(b) The peace officer verifies through the law enforcement information network that the individual is licensed under this act to carry a concealed pistol.

(8) As used in this section, "peace officer" includes a motor carrier officer appointed under section 6d of 1935 PA 59, MCL 28.6d, and security personnel employed by the state under section 6c of 1935 PA 59, MCL 28.6c.

EXHIBIT 11 A BAN ON TRANSPORTING LOADED FIREARMS OTHER THAN PISTOLS IN VEHICLES
MCL 750.227c Transporting or possessing loaded firearm in or upon vehicle; violation as misdemeanor; penalty; applicability to person violating MCL 312.10(1)(g).
Sec. 227c.
(1) Except as otherwise permitted by law, a person shall not transport or possess in or upon a sailboat or a motor vehicle, aircraft, motorboat, or any other vehicle propelled by mechanical means, a firearm, other than a pistol, which is loaded.

112

(2) A person who violates this section is guilty of a misdemeanor, punishable by imprisonment for not more than 2 years, or a fine of not more than $2,500.00, or both.

(3) This section does not apply to a person who violates section 10(1)(g) of chapter II of Act No. 286 of the Public Acts of 1929, as amended, being section 312.10 of the Michigan Compiled Laws.

History: Add. 1981, Act 103, Eff. Mar. 31, 1982

EXHIBIT 12 A DISORDERLY PERSONS LAW
MCL 750.167 "Disorderly person" defined;
subsequent violations by person convicted of
refusing or neglecting to support family.
Sec. 167.

(1) A person is a **disorderly** person if the person is any of the following:

(a) A person of sufficient ability who refuses or neglects to support his or her family.

(b) A common prostitute.

(c) A window peeper.

(d) A person who engages in an illegal occupation or business.

(e) A person who is intoxicated in a public place and who is either endangering directly the safety of another person or of property or is acting in a manner that causes a public disturbance.

(f) A person who is engaged in indecent or obscene conduct in a public place.

(g) A vagrant.

(h) A person found begging in a public place.

(i) A person found loitering in a house of ill fame or

prostitution or place where prostitution or lewdness is practiced, encouraged, or allowed.

(j) A person who knowingly loiters in or about a place where an illegal occupation or business is being conducted.

(k) A person who loiters in or about a police station, police headquarters building, county jail, hospital, court building, or other public building or place for the purpose of soliciting employment of legal services or the services of sureties upon criminal recognizance's.

(l) A person who is found jostling or roughly crowding people unnecessarily in a public place.

(2) When a person, who has been convicted of refusing or neglecting to support his or her family under this section, is then charged with subsequent violations within a period of 2 years, that person shall be prosecuted as a second offender, or third and subsequent offender, as provided in section 168, if the family of that person is then receiving public relief or support.

EXHIBIT 13 A HOW TO TRANSPORT NON-PISTOLS
MCL 750.227d Transporting or possessing firearm in or upon motor vehicle or self-propelled vehicle designed for land travel; conditions; violation as misdemeanor; penalty.

Sec. 227d.

(1) Except as otherwise permitted by law, a person shall not transport or possess in or upon a motor vehicle or any self-propelled vehicle designed for land travel a firearm, other than a pistol, unless the firearm is

unloaded and is 1 or more of the following:

(a) Taken down.

(b) Enclosed in a case.

(c) Carried in the trunk of the vehicle.

(d) Inaccessible from the interior of the vehicle.

(2) A person who violates this section is guilty of a misdemeanor, punishable by imprisonment for not more than 90 days, or a fine of not more than $100.00, or both.

EXHIBIT 14 A WEAPONS BAN
MCL 750.224 Weapons; manufacture, sale, or possession as felony; violation as felony; penalty; exceptions; "muffler" or "silencer" defined.

Sec. 224.

(1) A person shall not manufacture, sell, offer for sale, or possess any of the following:

(a)A machine gun or firearm that shoots or is designed to shoot automatically more than 1 shot without manual reloading, by a single function of the trigger.

(b)A muffler or silencer.

(c)A bomb or bombshell.

(d)A blackjack, slungshot, billy, metallic knuckles, sand club, sand bag, or bludgeon.

(e)A device, weapon, cartridge, container, or contrivance designed to render a person temporarily or permanently disabled by the ejection, release, or emission of a gas or other substance.

115

(2) A person who violates subsection (1) is guilty of a felony, punishable by imprisonment for not more than 5 years, or a fine of not more than $2,500.00, or both.

(3) Subsection (1) does not apply to any of the following:

(f)A self-defense spray or foam device as defined in section 224d.

(g)A person manufacturing firearms, explosives, or munitions of war by virtue of a contract with a department of the government of the United States.

(h)A person licensed by the secretary of the treasury of the United States or the secretary's delegate to manufacture, sell, or possess a machine gun, or a device, weapon, cartridge, container, or contrivance described in subsection (1).

(4) As used in this chapter, "muffler" or "silencer" means 1 or more of the following:

(i)A device for muffling, silencing, or deadening the report of a firearm.

(j)A combination of parts, designed or redesigned, and intended for use in assembling or fabricating a muffler or silencer.

(k)A part, designed or redesigned, and intended only for use in assembling or fabricating a muffler or silencer.

EXHIBIT 15 A SBS/SBR BAN
MCL 750.224b Short-barreled shotgun or rifle; manufacture, sale, or possession as felony; penalty; exceptions; applicability to collector's item.

Sec. 224b.

(1) A person shall not manufacture, sell, offer for sale, or possess a short-barreled shotgun or a short-barreled rifle.

(2) A person who violates this section is guilty of a felony punishable by imprisonment for not more than 5 years or a fine of not more than $2,500.00, or both.

(3) This section does not apply to the sale, offering for sale, or possession of a short-barreled rifle or a short-barreled shotgun which the secretary of the treasury of the United States of America, or his or her delegate, under 26 USC, sections 5801 through 5872, or 18 USC, sections 921 through 928, has found to be a curio, relic, antique, museum piece, or collector's item not likely to be used as a weapon, but only if the person selling, offering for sale or possessing the firearm has also fully complied with section 2 or 2a of 1927 PA 372, MCL 28.422 and 28.422a.

Section 20 of chapter 16 of the code of criminal procedure, 1927 PA 175, MCL 776.20, applies to this subsection.

EXHIBIT 16 A EAVESDROPPING
MCL 750.539c Eavesdropping upon private conversation.

Sec. 539c.

Any person who is present or who is not present during a private conversation and who wilfully uses any device to eavesdrop upon the conversation without the consent of all parties thereto, or who knowingly aids, employs or procures another person to do the same in violation of this section, is guilty of a felony punishable by imprisonment in a state prison for not more than 2 years or by a fine of not more than $2,000.00, or both.

EXHIBIT 17 A EAVESDROPPING DEFINITIONS MCL 750.539a Definitions.

Sec. 539a.

As used in sections 539a to 539i:

(1) "Private place" means a place where one may reasonably expect to be safe from casual or hostile intrusion or surveillance but does not include a place to which the public or substantial group of the public has access.

(2) "Eavesdrop" or "eavesdropping" means to overhear, record, amplify or transmit any part of the private discourse of others without the permission of all persons engaged in the discourse. Neither this definition or any other provision of this act shall modify or affect any law or regulation concerning interception, divulgence or recording of messages transmitted by communications common carriers.

(3) "Surveillance" means to secretly observe the activities of another person for the purpose of spying upon and invading the privacy of the person observed.

(4) "Person" means any individual, partnership, corporation or association.

EXHIBIT 18 A FOIA ACT

Act 442 of 1976 is Michigan's FOIA law. It is much too long to put in its entirety here. Even with the chapter on FOIA's and the excellent sample format, it is very important to look it up when issuing a PD a FOIA request, so that you are sure that you have all of the details right.

EXHIBIT 19 A CONCEALED CARRY FREE ZONES

MCL 28.425o Premises on which carrying concealed weapon prohibited; "premises" defined; exceptions to subsection (1); violation; penalties.

Sec. 5o.

(1)Subject to subsection (4), an individual licensed under this act to carry a concealed pistol, or who is exempt from licensure under section 12a(1)(f), shall not carry a concealed pistol on the premises of any of the following:

(a)A school or school property except that a parent or legal guardian of a student of the school is not precluded from carrying a concealed pistol while in a vehicle on school property, if he or she is dropping the student off at the school or picking up the child from the school. As used in this section, "school" and "school property" mean those terms as defined in section 237a of the Michigan penal code, 1931 PA 328, MCL 750.237a.

(b)A public or private child care center or day care center, public or private child caring institution, or public or private child placing agency.

(c)A sports arena or stadium.

(d)A bar or tavern licensed under the Michigan liquor control code of 1998, 1998 PA 58, MCL 436.1101 to 436.2303, where the primary source of income of the business is the sale of alcoholic liquor by the glass and consumed on the premises. This subdivision does not apply to an owner or employee of the business. The Michigan liquor control commission shall develop and make available to holders of licenses under the Michigan liquor control code of 1998, 1998 PA 58, MCL 436.1101 to 436.2303, an appropriate sign stating that "This establishment prohibits patrons from carrying concealed weapons". The owner or operator of an establishment licensed under the Michigan liquor control code of 1998, 1998 PA 58, MCL 436.1101 to 436.2303, may, but is not required to, post the sign developed under this subdivision. A record made available by an establishment licensed under the Michigan liquor control code of 1998, 1998 PA 58, MCL 436.1101 to 436.2303, necessary to enforce this subdivision is exempt from disclosure under the freedom of information act, 1976 PA 442, MCL 15.231 to 15.246.

(e)Any property or facility owned or operated by a church, synagogue, mosque, temple, or other place of worship, unless the presiding official or officials of the church, synagogue, mosque, temple, or other place of worship permit the carrying of concealed pistol on that property or facility.

(f)An entertainment facility with a seating capacity of 2,500 or more individuals that the individual knows or should know has a seating capacity of 2,500 or more individuals or that has a sign above each public entrance stating in letters not less than 1-inch high a seating capacity of 2,500 or more individuals.

(g)A hospital.

(h)A dormitory or classroom of a community college, college, or university.

(3) An individual licensed under this act to carry a concealed pistol, or who is exempt from licensure under section 12a(1)(f), shall not carry a concealed pistol in violation of R 432.1212 or a successor rule of the Michigan administrative code promulgated under the Michigan gaming control and revenue act, 1996 IL 1, MCL 432.201 to 432.226.

(4) As used in subsection (1), "premises" does not include parking areas of the places identified under subsection (1).

(5) Subsection (1) does not apply to any of the following:

(i)An individual licensed under this act who is a retired police officer or retired law enforcement officer. The concealed weapon licensing board may require a letter from the law enforcement agency stating that the retired police officer or law enforcement officer retired in good standing.

(j)An individual who is licensed under this act and who is employed or contracted by an entity described under subsection (1) to provide security services and is required by his or her employer or the terms of a contract to carry a concealed firearm on the premises of the employing or contracting entity.

(k)An individual who is licensed as a private investigator or private detective under the professional investigator licensure act, 1965 PA 285, MCL 338.821 to 338.851.

(l)An individual who is licensed under this act and who is a corrections officer of a county sheriff's department.

(m)An individual who is licensed under this act and who is a motor carrier officer or capitol security officer of the department of state police.

(n)An individual who is licensed under this act and who is a member of a sheriff's posse.

(o)An individual who is licensed under this act and who is an auxiliary officer or reserve officer of a police or sheriff's department.

(p)An individual who is licensed under this act and who is a parole or probation officer of the department of corrections.

(q)A state court judge or state court retired judge who is licensed under this act. The concealed weapon licensing board may require a state court retired judge to obtain and carry a letter from the judicial tenure commission stating that the state court retired judge is in good standing as authorized under section 30 of article VI of the state constitution of 1963, and rules promulgated under that section, in order to qualify under this subdivision.

(6) An individual who violates this section is responsible for a state civil infraction or guilty of a crime as follows:

(r)Except as provided in subdivisions (b) and (c), the individual is responsible for a state civil infraction and may be fined not more than $500.00. The court shall order the individual's license to carry a concealed pistol suspended for 6 months.

(s)For a second violation, the individual is guilty of a misdemeanor punishable by a fine of not more than $1,000.00. The court shall order the individual's license to carry a concealed pistol revoked.

(t)For a third or subsequent violation, the individual is guilty of a felony punishable by imprisonment for not more than 4 years or a fine of not more than $5,000.00, or both. The court shall order the individual's license to carry a concealed pistol revoked.

EXHIBIT 20 A LEIN SYSTEM RULES
28.214 Council; powers and duties; fingerprints; disclosure of information; violation; penalty.

Sec. 4.

(1) The council shall do all of the following:

(a) Establish policy and promulgate rules governing access, use, and disclosure of information in criminal justice information systems, including the law enforcement information network, the automated fingerprint information system, and other information systems related to criminal justice or law enforcement. The policy and rules shall do all of the following:

(i) Ensure access to information obtained by a federal, state, or local governmental agency to administer criminal justice or enforce any law.

(ii) Ensure access to information provided by the law enforcement information network or the automated fingerprint identification system by a governmental agency engaged in the enforcement of child support laws, child protection laws, or vulnerable adult protection laws.

(iii) Authorize a fire chief of an organized fire department or his or her designee to request and receive information obtained through the law enforcement information network by a law enforcement agency for the following purposes:

(A) A preemployment criminal convictions history.

(B) A preemployment driving record.

(C) Vehicle registration information for vehicles involved in a fire or hazardous materials incident.

(iv) Authorize a public or private school superintendent, principal, or assistant principal to receive vehicle registration information, of a vehicle within 1,000 feet of school property, obtained through the law enforcement information network by a law enforcement agency.

(v) Establish fees for access, use, or dissemination of information from criminal justice information systems.

(b) Review applications for C.J.I.S. access and approve or disapprove the applications and the sites. If an application is disapproved, the applicant shall be notified in writing of the reasons for disapproval.

(c) Establish minimum standards for equipment and software and its installation.

(d) Advise the governor on issues concerning the criminal justice information systems.

(2) A person having direct access to nonpublic information in the information systems governed by this act shall submit a set of fingerprints for comparison with state and federal criminal history records to be approved for access pursuant to the C.J.I.S. security

policy. A report of the comparison shall be provided to that person's employer.

(3) A person shall not access, use, or disclose nonpublic information governed under this act for personal use or gain.

(4) The attorney general or his or her designee, a prosecuting attorney, or the court, in a criminal case, may disclose to the defendant or the defendant's attorney of record information pertaining to that defendant that was obtained from the law enforcement information system.

(5) A person shall not disclose information governed under this act in a manner that is not authorized by law or rule.

(6) A person who intentionally violates subsection (3) or (5) is guilty of a crime as follows:

(a) For a first offense, the person is guilty of a misdemeanor punishable by imprisonment for not more than 93 days or a fine of not more than $500.00, or both.

(b) For a second or subsequent offense, the person is guilty of a felony punishable by imprisonment for not more than 4 years or a fine of not more than $2,000.00, or both.

EXHIBIT 21 A CC RESTRICTIONS
MCL 750.227 Concealed weapons; carrying; penalty.

Sec. 227.

(1) A person shall not carry a dagger, dirk, stiletto, a

double-edged nonfolding stabbing instrument of any length, or any other dangerous weapon, except a hunting knife adapted and carried as such, concealed on or about his or her person, or whether concealed or otherwise in any vehicle operated or occupied by the person, except in his or her dwelling house, place of business or on other land possessed by the person.

(2) A person shall not carry a pistol concealed on or about his or her person, or, whether concealed or otherwise, in a vehicle operated or occupied by the person, except in his or her dwelling house, place of business, or on other land possessed by the person, without a license to carry the pistol as provided by law and if licensed, shall not carry the pistol in a place or manner inconsistent with any restrictions upon such license.

(3) A person who violates this section is guilty of a felony, punishable by imprisonment for not more than 5 years, or by a fine of not more than $2,500.00.

EXHIBIT 22 A AIRPORT CARRY BAN

- MCL 259.80f Possessing... certain items in sterile area of airport;
   (1) An individual shall not possess, carry, or attempt to possess or carry any of the following in a sterile area of a commercial airport:
   (a) Firearm.
   (b) Explosive.
   (c) Knife with a blade of any length.
   (d) Razor, box cutter, or item with a similar blade.
   (e) Dangerous weapon.

(2) Except as provided in subsection (3), an individual who violates subsection (1) is guilty of a misdemeanor punishable by imprisonment for not more than 1 year or a fine of not more than $1,000.00, or both.

(3) An individual who violates subsection (1) while doing any of the following is guilty of a felony punishable by imprisonment for not more than 10 years or a fine of not more than $10,000.00, or both:

(a) Getting on or attempting to get on an aircraft.

(b) Placing, attempting to place, or attempting to have placed on an
    aircraft an item listed in subsection (1).

(c) Committing or attempting to commit a felony.

(4) [Exempts most officials]...

(7) As used in this section:

(a) 'Commercial airport' means an airport that has regularly scheduled commercial flights to and from other destinations.

(c) 'Sterile area' means that term as defined in 14 C.F.R. 107.1.

History: Add. 2001, Act 225, Eff. Apr. 1, 2002 .

EXHIBIT 23 A GAME AREA CARRY RULES
324.43510 Carrying or transporting firearm, slingshot, bow and arrow, crossbow or trap; license required; exception; applicability to taking of wild animal.
Sec. 43510.

(1) Subject to subsection (2) and except as provided in section 43513, a person shall not carry or transport a firearm, slingshot, bow and arrow, crossbow, or a trap while in any area frequented by wild animals unless that

person has in his or her possession a license as required under this part.

(2) This act or a rule promulgated or order issued by the department or the commission under this act shall not be construed to prohibit a person from transporting a pistol or carrying a loaded pistol, whether concealed or not, if either of the following applies:

(a) The person has in his or her possession a license to carry a concealed pistol under 1927 PA 372, MCL 28.421 to 28.435.

(b) The person is authorized under the circumstances to carry a concealed pistol without obtaining a license to carry a concealed pistol under 1927 PA 372, MCL 28.421 to 28.435, as provided for under any of the following:

(i) Section 12a of 1927 PA 372, MCL 28.432a.

(ii) Section 227, 227a, 231, or 231a of the Michigan penal code, 1931 PA 328, MCL 750.227, 750.227a, 750.231, and 750.231a.

(3) Subsection (2) does not authorize an individual to take or attempt to take a wild animal except as provided by law.

EXHIBIT 24 A BRANDISHING
MCL 750.234e
Brandishing **firearm in public; applicability; violation as misdemeanor; penalty.**

Sec. 234e.

(1) Except as provided in subsection (2), a person shall not knowingly brandish a firearm in public.

(2) Subsection (1) does not apply to any of the following:

(a) A peace officer lawfully performing his or her duties as a peace officer.

(b) A person lawfully engaged in hunting.

(c) A person lawfully engaged in target practice.

(d) A person lawfully engaged in the sale, purchase, repair, or transfer of that firearm.

(3) A person who violates this section is guilty of a misdemeanor punishable by imprisonment for not more than 90 days, or a fine of not more than $100.00, or both.

EXHIBIT 25 A CARRYING CONCEALED WEAPONS PENALTY
750.227 Concealed weapons; carrying; penalty.

Sec. 227.

(1) A person shall not carry a dagger, dirk, stiletto, a double-edged nonfolding stabbing instrument of any length, or any other dangerous weapon, except a hunting knife adapted and carried as such, concealed on or about his or her person, or whether concealed or otherwise in any vehicle operated or occupied by the person, except in his or her dwelling house, place of business or on other land possessed by the person.

(2) A person shall not carry a pistol concealed on or about his or her person, or, whether concealed or otherwise, in a vehicle operated or occupied by the

person, except in his or her dwelling house, place of business, or on other land possessed by the person, without a license to carry the pistol as provided by law and if licensed, shall not carry the pistol in a place or manner inconsistent with any restrictions upon such license.

(3) A person who violates this section is guilty of a felony, punishable by imprisonment for not more than 5 years, or by a fine of not more than $2,500.00.

APPENDIX B: ATTORNEY GENERAL OPINIONS

EXHIBIT 1 B
Office of the Attorney General
State of Michigan
Opinion No. 3158
February 14, 1945

CONCEALED WEAPONS - General discussion relative to concealed
weapons.

Mr. Clyde H. Edgar, Sheriff, Jackson County, Jackson
MI
Dear Sir:
Your letter addressed to the Michigan State Police and dated January 31, 1945 has been referred to me for reply. In your letter you ask substantially the following questions on weapons or firearms:

1. Is a weapon considered concealed when carried in a holster outside of all the clothing of a Person?
2. Is it necessary to have a license to carry a concealed pistol when such pistol is being transported from a city home to a place in the country, each of which places is owned by the party transporting the pistol, when the purpose of such transportation is target practice? Would the answer be the same if the place to which the pistol was being transported was owned by a near relative?

3. If a pistol is carried concealed or openly, with clip or cylinder removed, must a license be obtained?
4. A number of our local factories hire men for guard work only and furnish them with guns while on duty only. Is it necessary for them to have licenses to carry such guns?

The late Wm. W. Potter rendered an **opinion** in April of 1927 on the subject of your first questions and I quote the following from that **opinion**:

"The statute does not mean or import that no part of the weapons should be concealed, but the offense is only committed when the weapon is so concealed that it is impossible for one approaching in view of the person carrying the weapon to see any part of it. All that the Legislature meant when it prohibited the carrying of concealed weapons was to compel persons to so wear them that others who might come in contact with them might see that they were armed and dangerous persons, who were to be avoided in consequence, for, if it should be required that no part of the weapon should be concealed, the statute would amount to an infringement of the constitutional right of citizens to have and bear arms, since it would be impossible for one to have and bear about his person a pistol or weapon of any kind without having some part of it concealed. (Stockdale v. State, 32 Ga. 225, 227).

"I am, therefore, of the opinion that if a pistol is carried in a holster or belt, on the outside of the clothing so as to be in plain view, it does not constitute carrying a concealed weapon. If it is worn under a coat, it would be, in my judgment, a violation of the statute, as the same would then not be in plain view."

I agree with the conclusions reached in that opinion.

Relative to your second question, it is my opinion that Section 231 of Chapter 27 of the penal Code of the State of Michigan (Sec.28.428, Mich. Stat. Ann.) fairly defines the exceptions to the licensing act and therefore it is quoted:
"The provisions of the second, third, sixth and seventh sections of this chapter shall not apply to any peace officer of the state or any subdivision thereof who is regularly employed and paid by the state or such subdivisions, or to any member of the army, navy or marine corps of the United States or of organizations authorized by law to purchase or receive weapons from the United States or from this state, nor to the national guard or other duly authorized military organizations when on duty or drill, nor the members
thereof in going to or returning from their customary places of assembly or practice, nor by another state, nor to the regular and ordinary transportation of pistols as merchandise, or to any person while carrying a pistol unloaded in a wrapper from the place of purchase to his home or place of business or to a place of repair or back to his home or place of business, or in moving goods from one place of abode or business to another."
This section does not except the case of a person transporting a pistol from his city to his country home for target practice and it is therefore my opinion that it would be illegal to do so without the license to carry concealed weapons. The same would certainly be true

in case the pistol was being transported to a place owned by a near relative.

Answering your third question, it is my opinion that, if carried, openly, no license would be required since the weapon would not be concealed. However, if carried concealed, a license would be required regardless of whether the clip or cylinder were removed.

People v. Williamson, 200 Mich. 342.

Replying to your fourth question, Opinion No. 0-926, dated July 6, 1943, copy of which is enclosed, relative to plant protection men who are members of the auxiliary military police, seems to cover that situation adequately. However, as to plant protection men who are not members of military police auxiliary, it is my opinion that a license to carry concealed weapons is required. No license would be required if the weapons are carried openly.

Very truly yours,

JOHN R. DETHMERS
Attorney General

EXHIBIT 2 B LICENSED CARRY IN PISTOL FREE ZONES

STATE OF MICHIGAN

JENNIFER M. GRANHOLM, ATTORNEY GENERAL

A private investigator licensed to carry a concealed pistol is not, by reason of section 234d of the Michigan Penal Code, exempt from the gun-free zone restrictions imposed by section 5o of the Concealed Pistol Licensing Act.

Opinion No. 7097

January 11, 2002

Honorable Doug Spade
State Representative
The Capitol
Lansing, MI

You have asked whether a private investigator licensed to carry a concealed pistol is, by reason of section 234d of the Michigan Penal Code, exempt from the gun-free zone restrictions imposed by section 5o of the Concealed Pistol Licensing Act.

Private investigators are licensed under the Private Detective License Act of 1965, 1965 PA 285, MCL 338.821 *et seq*. That act does not, however, authorize a private investigator to carry a concealed pistol.

In the Concealed Pistol Licensing Act (Act), 1927 PA 372,[1] MCL 28.421 *et seq*, the Legislature has addressed the licensing of persons to carry concealed pistols. Section 5b of the Act contains the requirements for obtaining a license to carry a concealed pistol. Under section 12a, various categories of persons, including peace officers, are made exempt from the requirements of section 5b for obtaining a license to carry a concealed pistol. There is, however, no exemption for private investigators in section 12a or in any other section of the Act. Thus, private investigators may carry concealed pistols only if they are licensed to do so under section

5b of the Act. Once licensed to carry a concealed pistol, private investigators are subject to the Act's restrictions in the same manner as any other person licensed to carry a concealed pistol.

In 2000 PA 381, the Legislature significantly amended the Concealed Pistol Licensing Act. New section 5b of the Act changed the requirements for obtaining a license to carry a concealed pistol. Under section 5b(7), a county concealed weapon licensing board "shall issue a license to an applicant" who meets the requirements of the Act. Once the board has issued a license, the license holder may, subject to exceptions stated in section 5o, carry a concealed pistol "anywhere in this state."

In section 5o, however, the Legislature enumerated certain so-called gun-free zones, i.e., premises where a person licensed to carry a concealed pistol shall not carry a concealed pistol.

> Sec. 5o (1) *An individual licensed under this act to carry a concealed pistol, . . . shall not carry a concealed pistol on the premises of any of the following*:

a) A school or school property . . . .

b) A public or private day care center, public or private child caring agency, or public or private child placing agency.

c) A sports arena or stadium.

d) A dining room, lounge, or bar area of a premises licensed under the Michigan liquor control code of

136

1998 . . . . This subdivision shall not apply to an owner or employee of the premises.

e) Any property or facility owned or operated by a church, synagogue, mosque, temple or other place of worship, unless the presiding official or officials of the church, synagogue, mosque, temple, or other place of worship permit the carrying of concealed pistol on that property or facility.

f) An entertainment facility [that has a seating capacity of 2,500 or more].

g) A hospital.

h) A dormitory or classroom of a community college, college, or university. [Emphasis added.]

Section 5o of the Act expressly prohibits persons licensed under the Act from carrying concealed pistols in the specified gun-free zones.[2] Nothing in section 5o or in any other section of the Act exempts private investigators from its prohibitions. A clear and unambiguous statement in a statute must be enforced as written according to its plain meaning. *Dean v Dep't of Corrections,* 453 Mich 448, 454; 556 NW2d 458 (1996). In such instances, statutory construction is neither required nor permitted; rather, the court must apply the statutory language as written. *Piper v Pettibone Corp,* 450 Mich 565, 572; 542 NW2d 269 (1995). Therefore, a person licensed to carry a concealed pistol, even if that person is a licensed private investigator, must obey section 5o of the Concealed Pistol Licensing Act and shall not carry a concealed pistol in any of the gun-free zones identified in the Act.

This conclusion is not affected by the provisions of section 234d of the Michigan Penal Code, 1931 PA 328, MCL 750.1 *et seq.* That statute prohibits certain persons from possessing firearms on certain types of premises as follows:

> Sec. 234d (1) Except as otherwise provided in subsection (2), a person shall not possess a firearm on the premises of any of the following:

a) A depository financial institution or a subsidiary or affiliate of a depository financial institution.

b) A church or other house of religious worship.

c) A court.

d) A theatre.

e) A sports arena.

f) A day care center.

g) A hospital.

h) An establishment licensed under the Michigan liquor control act, ...

(2) This section does not apply to any of the following:

a) A person who owns, or is employed by or contracted by, an entity described in subsection (1) if the possession of that firearm is to provide security services for that entity.

b) A peace officer.

c) *A person licensed by this state or another state to carry a concealed weapon.*

d) A person who possesses a firearm on the premises of an entity described in subsection (1) if that possession is with the permission of the owner or an agent of the owner of that entity. [Emphasis added.]

By its express terms, section 234d prohibits certain persons from carrying a firearm in the enumerated places but explicitly exempts from its prohibition "[a] person licensed by this state or another state to carry a concealed weapon." Thus, any person licensed to carry a concealed pistol, including a private investigator, is exempt from the gun-free zone restrictions imposed by section 234d of the Penal Code and may therefore possess firearms while on the types of premises listed in that statute.

When applied to a private investigator licensed to carry a concealed pistol, there is no inherent conflict between the gun-free zone provisions in section 234d of the Penal Code and those in section 5o of the Concealed Pistol Licensing Act. The former statute, which prohibits firearms in certain protected zones, does not apply to persons who are licensed to carry a concealed weapon.[3] The latter statute, which contains no exemptions, prohibits concealed weapon licensees from carrying a concealed pistol in certain protected gun-free zones. The legislative prohibition in section 5o of the Concealed Pistol Licensing Act is not diminished in any way by section 234d of the Penal Code. When statutes govern the same subject matter and are in *pari materia,* the court must endeavor to construe them harmoniously and to give them reasonable effect. *Speaker v State Administrative Bd,* 441 Mich 547, 568, 579; 495 NW2d 539 (1993).

It is my opinion, therefore, that a private investigator licensed to carry a concealed pistol is not, by reason of section 234d of the Michigan Penal Code, exempt from the gun-free zone restrictions imposed by section 5o of the Concealed Pistol Licensing Act.

JENNIFER M. GRANHOLM
Attorney General

[1] The Act was significantly revised by amendatory 2000 PA 381.

[2] A person with a license to carry a concealed pistol who carries a pistol on premises protected under section 5o(1)(a)-(h) of the Concealed Pistol Licensing Act is subject to the penalties in section 5o(3)(a)-(c) of the Act. These penalties include fines, license suspension or revocation, and for third time offenders, up to four years imprisonment.

[3] A similar statutory provision criminalizes the possession of weapons in school zones but expressly exempts certain persons, including persons licensed to carry a concealed weapon. MCL 750.237a.

EXHIBIT 3 B OPEN CARRY NOT BRANDISHING
ADD 7101

STATE OF MICHIGAN

JENNIFER M. GRANHOLM, ATTORNEY GENERAL

CRIMINAL LAW:	Reserve police officer
FIREARMS:	carrying exposed but
	holstered handgun is not
LAW ENFORCEMENT:	brandishing firearm in
PEACE OFFICERS:	violation of Michigan Penal
POLICE:	Code

A reserve police officer, by carrying a handgun in a
holster that is in plain view, does not violate section
234e of the Michigan Penal Code, which prohibits
brandishing a firearm in public.

Opinion No. 7101

February 6, 2002

Honorable Bill Bullard, Jr.
State Senator
The Capitol
Lansing, MI

You have asked if a reserve police officer, by carrying a
handgun in a holster that is in plain view, violates
section 234e of the Michigan Penal Code, which
prohibits brandishing a firearm in public.

The Michigan Penal Code, MCL 750.1 *et seq*, revises,
consolidates, and codifies the state's criminal statutes.
Section 234e(1) of the Code criminalizes[1] the
brandishing of a firearm in public as follows:

> (1) Except as provided in
> subsection (2), a person shall
> not knowingly brandish a

firearm in public.

Subsection (2) of the same section states that "[s]ubsection (1) does not apply to . . . [a] peace officer lawfully performing his or her duties as a peace officer." The term "peace officer" refers to members of governmental police forces who have been given broad, general authority by law to enforce and preserve the public peace. *People v Bissonette*, 327 Mich 349, 356; 42 NW2d 113 (1950). Most governmental police officers, i.e., officers who are employed by the state or its political subdivisions, possess such authority and are, therefore, "peace officers." 1 OAG, 1955, No 1891, p 72 (February 24, 1955); 2 OAG, 1958, No 3212, p 60 (February 21, 1958). Conversely, police officers such as motor carrier enforcement officers who possess only restricted or special enforcement authority do not meet this standard and therefore do not qualify as "peace officers." *People v Bissonette, supra*; OAG, 1987-1988, No 6530, p 362 (August 5, 1988). Thus, a reserve police officer with limited law enforcement authority would not qualify as a "peace officer" under subsection 2 of section 234e of the Michigan Penal Code. A reserve police officer with general law enforcement authority who is regularly employed would qualify as a "peace officer" under subsection (2) of section 234e. See OAG, 1973-1974, No 4792, p 78 (August 27, 1973), and OAG, 1979-1980, No 5806, p 1055 (October 28, 1980). Section 234e of the Michigan Penal Code does not define the crime of brandishing a firearm in public. The Michigan Criminal Jury Instructions, published by the Committee on Standard Criminal Jury Instructions, does not include a recommended jury instruction on brandishing a firearm. Research discloses that while the term "brandishing" appears in reported Michigan cases,[2] none of the cases define the term.

In the absence of any reported Michigan appellate court decisions defining "brandishing," it is appropriate to rely upon dictionary definitions. *People v Denio,* 454 Mich 691, 699; 564 NW2d 13 (1997). According to *The American Heritage Dictionary, Second College Edition (1982)*, at p 204, the term brandishing is defined as: "1. To wave or flourish menacingly, as a weapon. 2. To display ostentatiously. –n. A menacing or defiant wave or flourish." This definition comports with the meaning ascribed to this term by courts of other jurisdictions. For example, in *United States v Moerman,* 233 F3d 379, 380 (CA 6, 2000), the court recognized that in federal sentencing guidelines, "brandishing" a weapon is defined to mean "that the weapon was pointed or waved about, or displayed in a threatening manner."

Applying these definitions to your question, it is clear that a reserve police officer, regardless whether he or she qualifies as a "peace officer," when carrying a handgun in a holster in plain view, is not waving or displaying the firearm in a threatening manner. Thus, such conduct does not constitute brandishing a firearm in violation of section 234e of the Michigan Penal Code.

It is my opinion, therefore, that a reserve police officer, by carrying a handgun in a holster that is in plain view, does not violate section 234e of the Michigan Penal Code, which prohibits brandishing a firearm in public.

JENNIFER M. GRANHOLM
Attorney General

[1]Violation of this section is a misdemeanor punishable

by imprisonment for up to 90 days, or a fine of not more than $100, or both.

[2] See, for example: *People v Jones,* 443 Mich 88, 90; 504 NW2d 158 (1993), *People v Kreger,* 214 Mich App 549, 552; 543 NW2d 55 (1995), and *People v Stubbs,* 15 Mich App 453, 455; 166 NW2d 477 (1968).

EXHIBIT 4 B OUT OF STATE LICENSES AND MICHIGAN RESIDENTS

Opinion No. 6798

May 16, 1994

CONCEALED WEAPON LICENSE:

Michigan resident with a concealed weapon license acquired from another state

A Michigan resident may not carry a concealed pistol in Michigan if the resident has only acquired a license to carry a concealed pistol from another state.

Honorable David Jaye

State Representative

The Capitol

Lansing, MI

You have asked whether a Michigan resident may carry a concealed pistol in Michigan if the resident has only acquired a license to carry a concealed pistol from another state.

MCL 28.432a; MSA 28.98(1), provides:

> Section 6 [requiring a concealed weapon license to carry a concealed pistol] does not apply to:

(f) A person licensed to carry a pistol concealed upon his or her person issued by another state.

Similarly, MCL 750.231a; MSA 28.428(1), states:

(1) Section 227 [prohibiting carrying a concealed pistol without a license] does not apply to any of the following:

(a) To a person holding a valid license to carry a pistol concealed upon his or her person issued by another state except where the pistol is carried in non-conformance with a restriction appearing on the license.

The above-quoted statutory provisions clearly apply to a resident of another state that obtains a license to carry a concealed pistol in that state and then comes into the State of Michigan. The question is whether the exemption is also applicable to a Michigan resident that obtains a license to carry a concealed pistol from another state and, on that basis, claims an exemption from the requirements of Michigan's concealed weapon laws.

In section 6 of 1927 PA 372, MCL 28.426; MSA 28.93, the Legislature has established a comprehensive procedure for determining whether a Michigan resident should be issued a license to carry a pistol concealed on the person or in a vehicle operated or occupied by the applicant. Subsection (1) of section 6 provides:

The prosecuting attorney, the sheriff, and the director of the department of state police, or their respective authorized deputies, shall constitute boards exclusively authorized to issue a license to an applicant residing within their respective

145

counties, to carry a pistol concealed on the person and to carry a pistol, whether concealed or otherwise, in a vehicle operated or occupied by the applicant. The county clerk of each county shall be clerk of the licensing board, which board shall be known as the concealed weapon licensing board. A license to carry a pistol concealed on the person or to carry a pistol, whether concealed or otherwise, in a vehicle operated or occupied by the person applying for the license, shall not be granted to a person unless the person is 18 years of age or older, is a citizen of the United States, and has resided in this state 6 months or more. A license shall not be issued unless it appears that the applicant has good reason to fear injury to his or her person or property, or has other proper reasons, and is a suitable person to be licensed. A license shall not be issued to a person who was convicted of a felony or confined for a felony conviction in this state or elsewhere during the 8-year period immediately preceding the date of the application or was adjudged insane unless the person was restored to sanity and so declared by court order. [Emphasis added.]

Subsection (4) requires fingerprinting the applicant and sending the fingerprints to the Michigan Department of State Police and the Federal Bureau of Investigation to ascertain whether there has been a felony conviction or confinement for a felony conviction within the 8-year period. Subsection (5) provides that the concealed pistol license may be restricted, on the face of the license, consistent with the reasons the license was issued.

Under subsection (6), a concealed pistol license may not be issued for more than three years and a renewal may not be granted unless a new application is filed.

Michigan's appellate courts have consistently recognized that the Legislature has imposed comprehensive requirements an applicant must meet to obtain a concealed pistol license from a county gun board. In People v McFadden, 31 MichApp 512, 516; 188 NW2d 141 (1971), the court stated:

> Pursuant to constitutional requirements, the statute enumerates explicit criteria to guide the concealed weapon licensing board in processing applications. Thus, any suggestion that absence of standards creates a potential for arbitrary action lacks merit.

Subsequently, in Hanselman v Wayne County Weapon Bd, 419 Mich 168, 189; 351 NW2d 544 (1984), the Supreme Court declared:

> Each concealed weapon licensing board must determine "proper reason" and "suitability" based upon consideration of local needs and an exercise of its discretion. As the Court of Appeals recognized in Bay County Concealed Weapons Licensing Board v Gasta, 96 MichApp 784, 789-791; 293 NW2d 707 (1980), the Legislature intends the concealed weapon licensing boards to apply local and discretionary standards in deciding whether to grant an applicant a concealed weapon license:
>
> "The licensing board is comprised of one representative each from the County Prosecutor's

Office, the State Police, and the County Sheriff's Department. By creating a board composed of law enforcement officials and giving it the exclusive authority to issue, deny and revoke permits for concealed weapons, the Legislature has insured that an individual's perceived need to carry a concealed weapon will be evaluated in light of the experience and knowledge of community needs possessed by these local officials. The potential danger which a concealed weapon poses to the unsuspecting public justifies that licensing procedures be entrusted to a board comprised of law enforcement officials.

"In view of the inherent potential danger which accompanies the issuance of a permit to carry a concealed weapon, the licensing board as composed reflects the Legislature's intent that power to issue and revoke such [concealed weapon] licenses is properly placed with those professionals most able to assess community needs and problems in this area." [Emphasis added.]

There are many rules for interpreting statutes. The ultimate goal of all such rules is to ascertain and implement the legislative intent, even if the intent might appear in conflict with the literal language of the statute. People v Stoudemire, 429 Mich 262, 266; 414 NW2d 693 (1987). Also, statutes must be interpreted to avoid absurd consequences. Webster v Rotary Electric Steel Co, 321 Mich 526, 531; 33 NW2d 69 (1948).

Here, the Legislature has created local gun boards with the exclusive authority to issue concealed pistol licenses. The Legislature has imposed specific statutory requirements applicants must meet to obtain these licenses. In addition, whether applicants have good reasons and are suitable persons to be licensed is within the sound discretion of a board of local professionals who apply their knowledge of community needs and problems in evaluating applications. It is inconceivable that the Legislature, after crafting these statutory requirements for obtaining a concealed pistol license, intended to permit Michigan residents to avoid them by obtaining a concealed pistol license in another state that may not impose many of the Michigan requirements. That construction of the statute would result in the absurd consequence that a Michigan resident could avoid the legislatively imposed requirements for obtaining a concealed pistol license in Michigan by obtaining that type of license in another state without having to meet the Michigan requirements. Thus, it must be concluded that a Michigan resident with a concealed pistol license obtained in another state may not carry a concealed pistol in Michigan unless the resident first obtains a concealed pistol license in Michigan by meeting the requirements for obtaining the license imposed by Michigan law.

It is my opinion, therefore, that a Michigan resident may not carry a concealed pistol in Michigan if the resident has only acquired a license to carry a concealed pistol from another state.

Frank J. Kelley
Attorney General

APPENDIX C: STATE LAWS NOT SPECIFICALLY REGARDING FIREARMS

EXHIBIT 1 C

MCL750.226... Carrying with unlawful intent

Any person who, with intent to use the same unlawfully against the person of another, goes armed with a pistol or other firearm or dagger, dirk, razor, stiletto, or knife having a blade over 3 inches in length, or any other dangerous or deadly weapon or instrument, shall be guilty of a felony, punishable by imprisonment in the state prison for not more than 5 years or by a fine of not more than 2,500 dollars.

EXHIBIT 2 C

- MCL 750.226a. Pocket knife opened by mechanical device...

Any person who shall sell or offer to sell, or any person who shall have in his possession any knife

having the appearance of a pocket knife, the blade or blades of which can be opened by a flick of a button, pressure on a handle or other mechanical contrivance shall be guilty of a misdemeanor... [Also, concealed carry may be charged as a felony under 750.227.] The provisions of this section [750.226a] shall not apply to any one-armed person carrying a knife on his person in connection with his living requirements.

EXHIBIT 3 C

-MCL 750.222a Double-edged, non-folding stabbing instrument defined.

(1) As used in this chapter, 'doubled-edged, non-folding stabbing instrument' does not include a knife, tool, implement, arrowhead, or artifact manufactured from stone by means of conchoidal fracturing.

(2) Subsection (1) does not apply to an item being transported in a vehicle, unless the item is in a container and inaccessible to the driver.

History: Add. 2000, Act 343, Imd. Eff. Dec. 27, 2000

EXHIBIT 4 C

-MCL 380.1313 Dangerous weapon found in possession of pupil...

(1) If a dangerous weapon is found in the possession of a pupil while the pupil is in attendance at school or a school activity or while the pupil is enroute to or from school on a school bus, the superintendent of the school district or intermediate school district, or his or her designee, immediately shall report that finding to the pupil's parent or legal guardian and the local law enforcement agency.

(2) If a school official finds that a dangerous weapon is in the possession of a pupil as described in subsection (1), the school official may confiscate the dangerous weapon or shall request a law enforcement agency to respond as soon as possible and to confiscate the dangerous weapon. If a school official confiscates a dangerous weapon under this subsection, the school official shall give the dangerous weapon to a law enforcement agency and shall not release the dangerous weapon to any other person, including the legal owner of the dangerous weapon. A school official who complies in good faith with this section is not
civilly or criminally liable for that compliance...

(4) As used in this section, 'dangerous weapon' means a firearm, dagger, dirk, stiletto, knife with a blade over 3 inches in length, pocket knife opened by a mechanical device, iron bar, or brass knuckles.

History: Add. 1987, Act 211, Imd. Eff. Dec. 22, 1987 ;--Am. 1995,

Act 76, Eff. Aug. 1, 1995 .

Popular Name: Act 451

Michigan Case Law:

- "Constitutionality: The double jeopardy protection against multiple punishment for the same offense is a restriction on a court's ability to impose punishment in excess of that intended by the Legislature, not a limit on the Legislature's power to define crime and fix punishment. People v. Sturgis, 427 Mich. 392, 397 N.W.2d 783 (1986).

- "Purpose of this section is to prevent quarreling or criminal persons from suddenly drawing weapons without notice to other persons." (1980)

- "Purpose of concealed weapons statutes, such as this section, is to prevent men in sudden quarrel or in commission of crime from drawing concealed weapons and using them without prior notice to their victims that they were armed, inasmuch as person attacked would behave one way if he knew his assailant was armed and perhaps another way if he could safely presume that assailant was unarmed." (1969)

- "The basic intent of the legislature as indicated in concealed weapon statute was that weapons should not

be carried when they might be used to take lives."
(1968)

_ "...the 'dwelling house' exception to the concealed
weapons statute did not apply to defendant who was
incarcerated in state prison at time of alleged
commission of such offense." (1978)

- "Purpose or intent with which a weapon is carried is
not an element of offense of carrying a concealed
weapon." (1973)- "Jury's determination that knife
sharpening steel, which defendant... contended he
carried only for protection... was a concealed weapon,
was justified." (1971)

- "Straight razor in pocket of defendant was
'concealed'..."
   (1967)

- "Daggers, dirks, stilettos... and similar articles,
designed for the purpose of bodily assault or defense,
are   generally recognized as 'dangerous weapons per
se'..." (1945)
- "Pocket knives, razors, hammers, hatchets, wrenches,
cutting tools, and other articles would constitute
   'dangerous weapons'... if used or carried for use as
weapons." (1945)

- "An ordinary jackknife with a pointed blade 3-5/16
inches long was not a 'dangerous weapon...' in the
absence of evidence that it was used or carried for use
as a weapon."(1945)

- "Five-inch, double-edged, non-folding knife was not a 'hunting knife' within hunting knife exception..." (1989)

- "Defendant charged with carrying concealed weapon had burden of proving that hunting knife was 'adapted and   carried as such'..." (1980)

APPENDIX D: CASE LAW

EXHIBIT 1 D
MCRGO V Ferndale

In 2002, the City of Ferndale passed an ordinance outlawing the carrying of any weapon on city property. This ordinance applied to all people other than police, and retired police. MCRGO promptly filed a court case challenging the ordinance. The local trial court agreed with the City but the Court of Appeals and the Michigan Supreme Court have reversed the trial court and clearly decided that a local unit of government has NO right to regulate the ownership, registration, purchase, sale, transfer, transportation, or possession of pistols or other firearms.

This case is a good example of the lengths that the people who want to take away our rights. After a unanimous three-judge decision from the Court of Appeals, the City attempted to file an appeal in the Michigan Supreme Court. The Supreme Court agreed with the MCRGO position and denied the City's attempt to appeal. The City filed more pleadings in the Court attempting to have the Court accept the case. The Supreme Court again denied the appeal.

EXHIBIT 2 D TERRY V OHIO

392 U.S. 1 (1968), was a decision by the United States Supreme Court which held that the Fourth Amendment prohibition on unreasonable searches and seizures is not

violated when a police officer stops a suspect on the street and searches him without probable cause to arrest, if the police officer has a reasonable suspicion that the person has committed, is committing, or is about to commit a crime.

For their own protection, police may perform a quick surface search of the person's outer clothing for weapons if they have reasonable suspicion that the person stopped is armed. This reasonable suspicion must be based on "specific and articulable facts" and not merely upon an officer's hunch. This permitted police action has subsequently been referred to in short as a "stop and frisk," or simply a "*Terry* stop". The *Terry* standard was later extended to temporary detentions of persons in vehicles, known as traffic stops.

The rationale behind the Supreme Court decision revolves around the understanding that, as the opinion notes, "the exclusionary rule has its limitations." The meaning of the rule is to protect persons from unreasonable searches and seizures aimed at *gathering evidence*, not searches and seizures for *other purposes* (like prevention of crime or personal protection of police officers).

EXHIBIT 3 D JL V Florida, SCOTUS 2000

In 1995 the Miami-Dade Police received an anonymous tip that a young black male was at a bus stop wearing a plaid shirt and carrying a firearm. The police went to the bus stop and saw three young black men, one wearing a plaid shirt. Acting solely on the tip (the officers did not observe any criminal or suspicious behavior), they searched all three, and found a pistol in the pocket of the man wearing the plaid shirt.

The trial court granted the juvenile defendant's motion to suppress evidence as fruit of an unreasonable search and seizure. However, the Florida Third District Court of Appeal reversed the trial court. J.L. appealed the decision to the Florida Supreme Court, which quashed the decision of the District Court, holding that the tip did not give sufficient indicia of reliability to justify a stop and frisk of the subject. The appellee sought certiorari review from the United States Supreme Court. Holding and rationale

The United States Supreme Court held in a unanimous opinion by Justice Ruth Bader Ginsburg that the search was unreasonable. That the tip accurately identified the defendant and that the allegation of the firearm ultimately proved to be accurate was insufficient to justify the seizure. For a completely anonymous tip to justify even a "stop and frisk" of a suspect pursuant to Terry v. Ohio, 392 U.S. 1 (1968), it must be "suitably corroborated" with both the accurate prediction of future activity of the subject[1] and accurate in its assertion of potential criminal activity. The tip given in the *J.L.* case was only sufficient to identify the subject and nothing more, making the police reliance upon it unjustified.

The Court further declined to create a standard "firearms exception" to the *Terry* doctrine, as was recognized in some Federal circuits, stating, among other things, that "Such an exception would enable any person seeking to harass another to set in motion an intrusive, embarrassing police search of the targeted person simply by placing an anonymous call falsely reporting the target's unlawful carriage of a gun.

APPENDIX E: FEDERAL LAWS

EXHIBIT 1 E GFSZA
TITLE 18 > PART I > CHAPTER 44 > § 922 922

(1) The Congress finds and declares that—

(A) crime, particularly crime involving drugs and guns, is a pervasive, nationwide problem;

(B) crime at the local level is exacerbated by the interstate movement of drugs, guns, and criminal gangs;

(C) firearms and ammunition move easily in interstate commerce and have been found in increasing numbers in and around schools, as documented in numerous hearings in both the Committee on the Judiciary [3] the House of Representatives and the Committee on the Judiciary of the Senate;

(D) in fact, even before the sale of a firearm, the gun, its component parts, ammunition, and the raw materials from which they are made have considerably moved in interstate commerce;

(E) while criminals freely move from State to State, ordinary citizens and foreign visitors may fear to travel to or through certain parts of the country due to concern about violent crime and gun violence, and parents may decline to send their children to school for the same reason;

(F) the occurrence of violent crime in school zones has resulted in a decline in the quality of education in our country;

(G) this decline in the quality of education has an adverse impact on interstate commerce and the foreign commerce of the United States;

(H) States, localities, and school systems find it almost

impossible to handle gun-related crime by themselves—even States, localities, and school systems that have made strong efforts to prevent, detect, and punish gun-related crime find their efforts unavailing due in part to the failure or inability of other States or localities to take strong measures; and

(I) the Congress has the power, under the interstate commerce clause and other provisions of the Constitution, to enact measures to ensure the integrity and safety of the Nation's schools by enactment of this subsection.

(A) It shall be unlawful for any individual knowingly to possess a firearm that has moved in or that otherwise affects interstate or foreign commerce at a place that the individual knows, or has reasonable cause to believe, is a school zone.

(B) Subparagraph (A) does not apply to the possession of a firearm—

(i) on private property not part of school grounds;

(ii) if the individual possessing the firearm is licensed to do so by the State in which the school zone is located or a political subdivision of the State, and the law of the State or political subdivision requires that, before an individual obtains such a license, the law enforcement authorities of the State or political subdivision verify that the individual is qualified under law to receive the license;

(iii) that is—

(I) not loaded; and

(II) in a locked container, or a locked firearms rack that is on a motor vehicle;

(iv) by an individual for use in a program approved by a school in the school zone;

(v) by an individual in accordance with a contract entered into between a school in the school zone and the individual or an employer of the individual;
(vi) by a law enforcement officer acting in his or her official capacity; or
(vii) that is unloaded and is possessed by an individual while traversing school premises for the purpose of gaining access to public or private lands open to hunting, if the entry on school premises is authorized by school authorities.

EXHIBIT 2 E NATIONAL PARK CARRY

512 of P.L. 111-24. Prohibits the Secretary of the Interior from promulgating or enforcing any regulation that prohibits an individual from possessing a firearm, including an assembled or functional firearm, in any unit of the National Park System (NPS) or the National Wildlife Refuge System (NWRS) if: (1) the individual is not otherwise prohibited by law from possessing the firearm; and (2) the possession of the firearm complies with the law of the state in which the NPS or NWRS unit is located.

EXHIBIT 3 E COLOR OF LAW CRIMES
Title 18, U.S.C., Section 242. Deprivation of Rights Under Color of Law

This statute makes it a crime for any person acting under color of law, statute, ordinance, regulation, or custom to willfully deprive or cause to be deprived from any person those rights, privileges, or immunities secured or protected by the Constitution and laws of the

U.S.

This law further prohibits a person acting under color of law, statute, ordinance, regulation or custom to willfully subject or cause to be subjected any person to different punishments, pains, or penalties, than those prescribed for punishment of citizens on account of such person being an alien or by reason of his/her color or race.

Acts under "color of any law" include acts not only done by federal, state, or local officials within the bounds or limits of their lawful authority, but also acts done without and beyond the bounds of their lawful authority; provided that, in order for unlawful acts of any official to be done under "color of any law," the unlawful acts must be done while such official is purporting or pretending to act in the performance of his/her official duties. This definition includes, in addition to law enforcement officials, individuals such as Mayors, Council persons, Judges, Nursing Home Proprietors, Security Guards, etc., persons who are bound by laws, statutes ordinances, or customs. Punishment varies from a fine or imprisonment of up to one year, or both, and if bodily injury results or if such acts include the use, attempted use, or threatened use of a dangerous weapon, explosives, or fire shall be fined or imprisoned up to ten years or both, and if death results, or if such acts include kidnapping or an attempt to kidnap, aggravated sexual abuse or an attempt to commit aggravated sexual abuse, or an attempt to kill, shall be fined under this title, or imprisoned for any term of years or for life, or both, or may be sentenced to death.

EXHIBIT 4 E COLOR OF LAW CIVIL ACTION
TITLE 42--Sec. 1983. Civil action for deprivation of rights

Every person who, under color of any statute, ordinance, regulation, custom, or usage, of any State or Territory or the District of Columbia, subjects, or causes to be subjected, any citizen of the United States or other person within the jurisdiction thereof to the deprivation of any rights, privileges, or immunities secured by the Constitution and laws, shall be liable to the party injured in an action at law, suit in equity, or other proper proceeding for redress, except that in any action brought against a judicial officer for an act or omission taken in such officer's judicial capacity, injunctive relief shall not be granted unless a declaratory decree was violated or declaratory relief was unavailable. For the purposes of this section, any Act of Congress applicable exclusively to the District of Columbia shall be considered to be a statute of the District of Columbia.

EXHIBIT 5 E 2ND AMENDMENT, BILL OF RIGHTS
A well regulated militia being necessary to the security of a free state, the right of the people to keep and bear arms shall not be infringed.

EXHIBIT 6 E 4TH AMENDMENT, BILL OF RIGHTS
4th Amendment, Bill Of Rights: The right of the people to be secure in their persons, houses, papers, and effects, against unreasonable searches and seizures,

shall not be violated, and no Warrants shall issue, but upon probable cause, supported by Oath or affirmation, and particularly describing the place to be searched, and the persons or things to be seized.

APPENDIX F: MSP LEGAL UPDATES ON OC

For further reference for the reader to get a third-party perspective, below are several recent MSP legal update newsletter segments regarding OCing.

MICHIGANSTATEPOLICE
LEGAL UPDATE
NO. 86
OCTOBER 26, 2010

FIREARMS LAW

As more and more police officers are encountering citizens who are openly carrying firearms in Michigan, the Michigan State Police offers this special edition of the Update to assist officers in familiarizing themselves with Michigan laws regarding both open and concealed carrying of firearms.

Open carry of firearms

In Michigan, it is legal for a person to carry a firearm in public as long as the person is carrying the firearm with lawful intent and the firearm is not concealed. You will not find a law that states it is legal to openly carry a firearm. It is legal because there is no Michigan law that prohibits it; however, Michigan law limits the premises on which a person may carry a firearm.

MCL 750.234d provides that it is a 90 day misdemeanor to possess a firearm on the premises of any of the following:

A depository financial institution (e.g., bank or credit union)
A church or other place of religious worship
A court
A theater
A sports arena
A day care center
A hospital
An establishment licensed under the Liquor Control Code

The above section does not apply to any of the following:
The owner or a person hired as security (if the firearm is possessed for the purpose of providing security)

A peace officer
A person with a valid concealed pistol license (CPL) issued by any state

164

A person who possesses on one of the above listed premises with the permission of the owner or owner's agent.

Officers must be aware of the above exemption for valid CPL holders as many of the citizens who openly carry firearms possess valid CPLs. An individual with a valid CPL may carry a non-concealed firearm in the above listed premises.

A CPL holder is not required by law to carry a pistol concealed. A CPL holder may carry a pistol concealed or non-concealed.

A private property owner has the right to prohibit individuals from carrying firearms on his or her property, whether concealed or otherwise, and regardless of whether the person is a CPL holder. If a person remains on the property after being told to leave by the owner, the person may be charged with trespassing (MCL 750.552).

MCL 750.226 states it is a felony for a person to carry a dangerous weapon, including a firearm, with the intent to use the weapon unlawfully against another person.

Possession of firearms in public by a minor is addressed in MCL 750.234f.

Brandishing firearms

MCL 750.234e provides that it is a 90-day misdemeanor for a person to knowingly brandish a firearm in public. Brandishing is not defined in Michigan law and there are no reported Michigan cases that define the term. Attorney General Opinion No. 7101 provides guidance and states, "A person when carrying a handgun in a holster in plain view is not waving or displaying the firearm in a threatening manner. Thus, such conduct does not constitute brandishing a firearm...."

Transporting firearms

Michigan law details how firearms may be transported in a vehicle. MCL 750.227c and MCL 750.227d discuss the transportation of firearms, other than pistols, in vehicles.

MCL 750.227(2) makes it a felony for a person to transport a pistol anywhere in a vehicle unless the person is licensed to carry a concealed

This update is provided for informational purposes only. Officers should contact their local prosecutor for an interpretation before applying the information contained in this update. MSP Legal Update No. 86 Page 2 of 3

pistol. Exceptions to the above statute are found in MCL 750.231a.

One such exception allows for transportation of pistols in a vehicle for a "lawful purpose." A lawful purpose includes going to or from any one of the following:

A hunting or target area
A place of repair
Moving goods from a home or business to another home or business
A law enforcement agency (for a safety inspection or to turn the pistol over to the agency)
A gun show or place of sale or purchase
A public shooting facility

Public land where shooting is legal
Private property where a pistol may be lawfully used

MCL 750.231a also provides that a pistol transported for a "lawful purpose" by a person not licensed to carry a concealed pistol must be all of the following:
Unloaded

In a closed case designed for firearms
In the trunk (or if the vehicle has no trunk, it must not be readily accessible to the occupants)
There is no way to "open carry" a pistol in a vehicle. An individual, without a CPL or otherwise exempted (e.g., a police officer), who transports a pistol in a vehicle to an area where he or she intends to "open carry" may be in violation of MCL 750.227.

Carrying concealed weapons
MCL 750.227 also makes it a felony for a person to carry a concealed pistol on or about his or her person unless the person is exempt under MCL 750.231 or MCL 750.231a. Complete invisibility is not required. The carrying of a pistol in a holster or belt outside the clothing is not carrying a concealed weapon. Carrying a pistol under a coat is carrying a concealed weapon. Op. Atty. Gen. 1945, O-3158. According to the Court of Appeals in *People v. Reynolds*, a weapon is concealed if it is not observed by those casually observing the suspect as people do in the ordinary course and usual associations of life. 38 Mich App. 159 (1970).

Firearms Act
MCL 28.422 provides that a person shall not purchase, carry, possess, or transport a pistol in Michigan without first having obtained a License to Purchase and registering the pistol. The statute contains exemptions for certain persons and additional exemptions are located in MCL 28.422a and in MCL 28.432.
A person with a valid Michigan CPL does not have to obtain a License to Purchase; however, he or she still has to register the pistol after he or she purchases or otherwise acquires it using a Pistol Sales Record (MCL 28.422a). Violation is a state civil infraction. Additionally, a person with a valid CPL can carry, possess, use, or transport a properly registered pistol belonging to another (MCL 28.432).
Pistol buyers are required to have in their possession their copy of the License to Purchase or Pistol Sales Record when carrying, using, possessing, and transporting the pistol for 30 days after they acquire the pistol. These records are commonly referred to as Registration Certificates or Green Cards. Officers are reminded that after 30 days, there is no requirement to have either record in their possession or to keep either record.
MCL 28.425o provides that a person with a valid CPL shall not carry a concealed pistol in a pistol-free zone. First offense is a state civil infraction.

The following is a list of the premises (excluding parking lots) included in the statute:

School or school property, except a parent or legal guardian who is dropping off or picking up a child and the pistol is kept in the vehicle
Public or private day care center
Sports arena or stadium
A bar or tavern where sale and consumption of liquor by the glass is the primary source of income (does not apply to owner or employee of the business).
Any property or facility owned or operated by a church, synagogue, mosque, temple, or other place of worship, unless authorized by the presiding official
An entertainment facility that has a seating capacity of 2,500 or more
A hospital
A dormitory or classroom of a community college, college, or university
A casino (R 432.1212, MCL 432.202)

Note, the above statute applies to CPL holders carrying a **concealed** pistol. If the CPL holder is carrying a non-concealed pistol, the statute does not apply. As noted above, the unlawful premises listed in MCL 750.234d do not apply to persons with a valid CPL. Therefore, a person with a valid CPL may carry a non-concealed pistol in the areas described in MCL 28.425o and MCL 750.234d.
Additionally, the above listed pistol-free zones for CPL holders do not apply to the following individuals when they are licensed to carry a concealed weapon:

Retired police officers
Persons employed or contracted by a listed entity to provide security where carrying a concealed pistol is a term of employment
Licensed private detectives or investigators
Sheriff's department corrections officers
State police motor carrier officers or capital security officers
Members of a sheriff's posse
Auxiliary or reserve officers of a police or sheriff's department
Parole or probation officers of the department of corrections
Current or retired state court judges

Out-of-state residents
Non-residents may legally possess a firearm more than 30 inches in length in Michigan. In order for a non-resident to possess a pistol in Michigan, he or she must either be licensed to carry a concealed pistol or be licensed by his or her state of residence to purchase, carry, or transport a pistol. The ownership of property in Michigan does not qualify a non-resident to possess a pistol in Michigan.
Non-resident concealed pistol possession

MCL 750.231a makes it legal for a non-resident of Michigan with a valid CPL issued by his or her state of residence to carry a concealed pistol in Michigan as long as the pistol is carried in conformance with any and all restrictions appearing on the license. Individuals with out of state CPLs are subject to Michigan laws that govern Michigan CPL holders. As many states issue CPLs to out of state residents, officers should verify that the person actually resides in the state that issued the license. If the person does not reside in the state that issued the license, Michigan does not recognize the CPL and the person may not carry a concealed pistol in Michigan.

Possession of pistols by non-residents
MCL 28.432 makes it legal for non-residents of Michigan who hold valid CPLs issued by another state to possess a non-concealed pistol in Michigan without complying with Michigan's pistol registration requirements. Additionally, MCL 28.422 exempts residents of other states from Michigan's pistol registration requirements therefore, allowing them to possess a pistol in Michigan, if all of the following requirements are met:
The person is licensed by his or her state of residence to purchase, transport, or carry a pistol,

The person is in possession of the license while in Michigan,
The person owns the pistol possessed in Michigan,
The person possesses the pistol for a lawful purpose as defined in MCL 750.231a, and
The person is in Michigan less than 180 days and does not intend to establish residency here.

A non-resident must present the license issued by his or her state of residence to a police officer upon demand. Failure to do so is a 90-day misdemeanor. When transporting a firearm in Michigan, non-residents must transport pistols in compliance with MCL 750.231a (discussed above in the Transporting Firearms section), unless they have a concealed pistol license issued by their state of residence.
Officers are reminded that the Fourth Amendment protects citizens from unreasonable searches and seizures. Carrying a non-concealed firearm is generally legal. Officers may engage in a consensual encounter with a person carrying a non-concealed pistol; however, in order to stop a citizen, officers are required to have reasonable suspicion that crime is afoot. For example, officers may not stop a person on the mere possibility the person may be carrying an unregistered pistol. Officers must possess facts rising to the level of reasonable suspicion to believe the person is carrying an unregistered pistol. Officers are also reminded there is no general duty for a citizen to identify himself or herself to a police officer unless the citizen is being stopped for a Michigan Vehicle Code violation.

168

APPENDIX INDEX

****APPENDIX A: STATE LAWS****

***APPENDIX B: ATTORNEY GENERAL
OPINIONS***

Licensed carry in "pistol free zones"; see page 124
-EXHIBIT 3 B Opinion No. 7101
Open carry not brandishing; see page 140
-EXHIBIT 4 B Opinion No. 6798
Out of state licenses and Michigan residents; see page 144

APPENDIX C: STATE LAWS ABOUT OTHER WEAPONS

-EXHIBIT 1 C Carrying with unlawful intent
MCL750.226; see page 150
-EXHIBIT 2 C Pocket knife opened by mechanical device
MCL750.226a; see page 150
-EXHIBIT 3 C Daggers
MCL 750.222a; see page 150
-EXHIBIT 4 C Weapons found on pupil in K-12 school
MCL 380.1313; see page 151

APPENDIX D: CASE LAW

-EXHIBIT 1 D
MCRGO V Ferndale; see page 155
-EXHIBIT 2 D
Terry v Ohio; see page 155
-EXHIBIT 3 D
JL V Florida, SCOTUS 2000; see page 156

CONDUCTING FURTHER RESEARCH

With the nearly universal access to the Internet that people enjoy in today's society, looking up laws is easier than ever. A visit to http://www.legislature.mi.gov/ will enable you to search the very latest information about Michigan bills and laws. Federal laws may be searched at http://uscode.house.gov/search/criteria.shtml The author encourages you to do your own research, and not rely solely on the information presented in this book.

LET US KNOW WHAT YOU THINK!

If you read this book and you have any suggestions about ways it can be improved, or if you know of something this book has wrong, we want to hear from you. This book is an attempt to answer every question someone could have about open carrying in Michigan. This is an enormous and complicated subject, and we know this book isn't without its faults. We will always strive to improve later editions. Please email comments to president@citizensleaguesd.com

QUIZ ANSWERS

1C 2B 3D 4A 5E 6A 7D 8E 9E 10C 11D 12D
13A 14D 15B 16E 17E 18A 19B